T0370365

SPEAKING
with the
ANCESTORS

KRISTIANNE FERRIER

BALBOA.PRESS
A DIVISION OF HAY HOUSE

Balboa Press books may be ordered through booksellers or by contacting:

Balboa Press
A Division of Hay House
1663 Liberty Drive
Bloomington, IN 47403
www.balboapress.com
844-682-1282

Because of the dynamic nature of the Internet, any web addresses or links contained in this book may have changed since publication and may no longer be valid. The views expressed in this work are solely those of the author and do not necessarily reflect the views of the publisher, and the publisher hereby disclaims any responsibility for them.

The author of this book does not dispense medical advice or prescribe the use of any technique as a form of treatment for physical, emotional, or medical problems without the advice of a physician, either directly or indirectly. The intent of the author is only to offer information of a general nature to help you in your quest for emotional and spiritual well-being. In the event you use any of the information in this book for yourself, which is your constitutional right, the author and the publisher assume no responsibility for your actions.

Any people depicted in stock imagery provided by Getty Images are models, and such images are being used for illustrative purposes only. Certain stock imagery © Getty Images.

This book is a work of non-fiction. Unless otherwise noted, the author and the publisher make no explicit guarantees as to the accuracy of the information contained in this book and in some cases, names of people and places have been altered to protect their privacy.

Print information available on the last page.

ISBN: 979-8-7652-4947-5 (sc)
ISBN: 979-8-7652-4946-8 (e)

Library of Congress Control Number: 2024902372

Balboa Press rev. date: 04/12/2024

CONTENTS

FORETHOUGHT

Grandfather Tobi told me about his granddaughter, Forest Woman, and how she would go outside, look at the moon, imagine the ancestors, and then she would travel with them. He visited me that day and said, "I am your grandfather, and your blood runs with ours." He also said to always *speak from the heart*. They were my Ojibwa Chippewa ancestors who lived over two hundred years ago. Forest Woman was my 4th Great-Grandmother. So how do I know all of this? Because, as I said, he told me so. He said my gift comes from my native side, although I suspect, it's not the only side.

The ancestors communicate with me in dreams and through meditation, and sometimes I hear the accents they spoke in that life.

After visiting my Revolutionary War 5th Great-Grandfather Colonel Richard's burial site and monument in Louisville, Kentucky, I came home through the garage and into my laundry room and heard a booming almost British voice say, "Lafayette, Lafayette, that rat bastard. The Taylor brothers saved his ass more than once."

My sister and I had discussed in the car and on the way home, about the Revolutionary War, and the young General Lafayette.

Over the years other things happened and I realized my abilities. I tried to understand them, studied parapsychology, and tried automatic writing, but never really felt like I had any major capabilities, plus, people feel funny talking about such things. People might look at you like you are crazy, but still, my interest did not wane.

Over fifteen years ago, I took my first meditation class and that class opened me up. I now teach meditation.

COMPLEXITIES
OF THE MIND

I WANTED TO START THIS by saying, that the reason I've delved so deep is because I seek answers, answers to the truth of why we are here. As I have gone deeper into my study of the mind, I've found the closer I am to my family on the other side, the more I become in tune with who I am, and this has made me even more curious, for when we realize how much the ancestors are a part of us, and understand their curious nature, then we can see why we have come to the earth school.

I call this chapter complexities of the mind because of the long conversation I had with a friend, Carl, who is an incredible psychiatrist. He's long given up his career, however, still teaches.

In writing this book, I was offered important advice from this advisor. Don't go overkill with this book, meaning, the ideas and stories will resonate with some, others will poo poo it, and call it unnecessary drivel, well, I say to them, isn't it intelligent to seek answers.

He furthered, in knowing this, of course, the punctuation must be perfect. You have other issues with this book. The lack of credibility.

So, I thought about this. I have told the world I communicate with spirits. Is that believable? Yes, it is. What do I have to back it up? Is there knowledge of these things? I am believable to some and the other side, however, I needed to back up what makes me believable to the readers of this book. I am talking about the ever-presence of spirits and their contributions.

People have what I like to call a practical mind, and in my book, for all purposes, I had no credence. So, in fixing this, I needed to do the things an author does when writing a non-fiction book by finding sources to prove that these things are true and next, by putting them into a source page that says, these are the resources I found to prove these happenings to be true.

I felt I would begin to see the light of day when I could say to myself, I did not imagine all these things, and when that happens, I can hold my head high and say, I told you so.

It's not impossible to find resources, just time-consuming, and frankly, well, for this kind of book, maybe not so relevant.

Extrapolate. The word extrapolate kept coming to mind and I knew this word was important to the work I am doing. The word has many meanings to it. When we have an idea, we do many things with it. We can generalize the idea and then broaden it to a conclusion. Based on what we know, we can allow ourselves to be open-minded, or we can devalue the very sense of knowledge based on what we know.

If we give credence to a thought or an idea, we can translate it into very basic logical other ideas until we come up with the final deduction. With this in mind, we can go further in our thoughts than we ever dreamed possible. In understanding this conception, we model ourselves after others. Translation meaning in layman's terms, we are broader-minded than we realize.

Fixed knowledge is only on the surface.

If you can devise a way to go deeper, that is to introduce a new way of thinking. To tap into that part of the brain that has been sorely neglected.

This book was originally being written to evolve the mind to speak with our ancestors, to communicate with those who came before us. To me, that didn't seem enough.

There is more to receiving outside knowledge.

A big part of my life is communicating with those who have moved on, and not only them but also communicating with my earth living compadres. To access and to gain knowledge from the fifth dimension, well, the very thought of revealing this is intimidating to say the least, however, they want us to be reminded of our heavenly existence, and if this is too much to take in, well, like I always say, baby steps. I confer with my advisors to reveal this slowly.

Take a minute, breathe in slowly, and acknowledge you are truly here, an actual living breathing being. You can connect with your five senses. And now, what if you could connect to another sense, the sense some refer to as the sixth sense? This sense is not out of our realm of reaching.

There are waves of information out there, waiting to be tapped into. This science, this wealth of information that others have transmitted into, which has brought about genius such as quantum physicists, mathematicians, and other far-thinking individuals who have seen into clearly other places. The waves of Alpha, Beta, and Theta that give us our answers.

Many of these geniuses are well known and others have not been given their fair share of the glory their contributions have made. I would surmise that there are many written accounts of their genius, their contributions to the mainstream.

Genius has long fascinated me, not that I am one, just the thought of someone from a young age who has defied logic and been given abilities others have not. What separated them from other children who did not possess the gift of understanding bigger ideas?

Well, we may never know all, it could be genetic, larger areas of the brain, it could be they were born to prosper where others had not. If this is the case, could it be with the right upbringing that we could find success, meaning if we are given the right encouragement at a young age, we could lead a life of prosperity. Could it be that they connected to a higher source?

I do know it is recorded that my fifth-great grandfather, Richard, saw to his children's education, even his daughters, and all in the wilderness of early Kentucky, where they were taught history and the Bible. They were given an education of knowledge from books, from holistic practices, maybe this is why my fourth great-grandfather, William, became a surgeon. They were given an education to further them on their life path, and some more than others achieved written-about successes.

I like to think I carry some of those genetics, although my education was lacking, lacking in what would cause me to sit up and think, to be given inspiration that could have driven me to succeed at a younger age.

I have to laugh, for maybe it's not too late for me if I tap into that universal stream, that road of knowledge.

My friend, Carl, told me, "The hypothesis of the mind is not quite what it seems. I categorize people in two ways. We have our inferior self and our notably higher self. These two sides conflict with one another. I correct myself by the way of integrating these two ways of thinking. Objectifying oneself into complacency reduces the life force within all of us. We are designed to be more than basic creatures; we are designed to be far advanced."

"So, where do we balance these two complexities of the mind? We counterbalance our thoughts along with our hearts. We can contribute to society our thoughts and minds. This isn't always easy, but in the long run, this is easier than having our combative mind in control."

"We are in two minds, and these two parts of thinking can become in harmony with one another, or not." I have found this true, not only with the living, but also, with the dead.

I thought about what Carl said. Of course, I would not have said it as brilliantly.

We criticize others for our own incompetencies, and these criticisms reflect badly on ourselves as well as others. Once we quit judging others, we can look inward at the judgments we hold on ourselves.

When it comes down to it, we judge ourselves more harshly than others judge us.

Gaze into your own eyes before you gaze into someone else's, for your own critic is more severe than the throng.

Altruism comes in many forms. We can give of ourselves a little, or we can give until it hurts. Any way you look at it, we can begin to see, we aren't here for ourselves.

Syed came to me one morning. I could hear his Indian accent. I am not a morning person by any means, and the fact another spirit came to me and wanted my full attention, irritated me. I made my way through the house and began to communicate with Syed. I asked him if he wanted to go to the light and he agreed. For the next few hours, I felt his energy around me. What he said broke my heart. He said he was a person in life who would not draw the attention of someone like me. He also said people are wastrels with their money. I never got his story of why he hadn't moved on, but he is finally home, and on the other side in his true form, not the insignificant person he was in life. He reminded me, we should not judge people by their outer shells.

Can the lowest street person be someone who deserves our care? When I met Syed, he came to me for help, so he could move on, and be with his family in his true home. That's what most of the spirits who contact me want, just to move on. I did not visually see Syed at first, however, he was cordial like many of the spirits who come to me. Later he showed me how he'd been disfigured at birth, living with a club foot and a cleft palate.

Withstanding, we all have relevance, we all have a purpose.

We also regard ourselves as pretty good judges of character, but are we? Do we not judge people on the clothes they wear, the car they drive, and quite possibly the career they work in? If we do, then maybe we need to look a little closer.

Those who judge and keep their chin fully in the air are missing the view down below.

In many societies, those with disabilities are treated as outcasts. Civilizations from the beginning of time have treated others with mental illness, disfigurement, homosexuality, and other maladies, as undesirable. We, ourselves, have probably lived a life or two as one of these people, for it takes a strong soul to take on one of these lives.

You as an individual have lived many lives. Some more than others.

My friend, Carl, is also a wonderful philosopher. He equates many of his studies to harken back to early modern society. He thinks about whimsical knowledge as a product of the human purpose.

We all have divinity in our purpose, so why not use this to our advantage? Why not take practical measures for our own reassurance against bigotry and demeaning others?

Let's look at judgment as a type of recourse.

When we judge others, we are losing our hold of who we are. We don't come here to judge, we come here to learn and to listen, listen to our heart.

Others can lose their way, and it is a humanistic purpose to help others on their path. Even if our path is slightly askew, we can still help guide others on their path to improvement. We spend too much time on ourselves, on our wants and desires that we forget to look around us and see that others are taking up Earth space also.

We can be a product of a degraded society that has devalued its citizens to promiscuous, often people devoid of any moral character development in such a way it can be destructive to innocent and decent citizens of the countries they live in.

We can be a product of our own making.

A people of possibilities who have devalued each other for so long, it is hard to even know how to come out of this way of thinking. If your action is destructive to someone else's soul, then stop. Think, how will I live with what I've done? Will I turn a blind eye to my destruction of someone else? If you do, then you destroy who you are.

I am not here to criticize anyone; I am saying these things to make you stop and listen to what your heart tells you is wrong or right. That inner voice that knows the truth, knows the truth of who you are, and not the damaged person who someone else inflicted their own damage upon, however, someone who can stop this influx of diseased thinking.

THE OPEN MIND

B ACK TO CARL, THE most amazing analyzer I've ever met. He began to analyze me.

I've analyzed you," he said, "and find you have an adept mind. Few like you have altered their thinking capacities to the open mind. The open mind is more adept at figuring out solutions. So, in terms of resilience, you have the capacity to reach new heights, and this is why it's important to reveal yourself to others. In doing so, you will teach others what has long been hidden."

As you have probably figured out, he is truly an open mind for a man of science.

He wants to make clear that revealing who you are is an example of regarding the human mind in its capacity to delve deeper. The knowledge you are given is a representation of who we all are. Why not encourage others to live by example?

I do creatively figure out answers. I think this is why my early experiences with the unexplainable drove my curiosity to seek explanations.

I came to the realization, I needed to resort to a new way of being. To retrain my primitive brain, which some refer to as the critter brain. I had to divide the objective part of my brain and the logical part of my brain. The part that said to keep these things quiet. The logical side told me that others like to be on the surface, including me at times. We've had implanted long time held onto ideas, keeping ourselves from seeing the truth.

The truth, I thought jokingly, could reveal terror among the masses. The truth in quantum physics that can explain black holes, wormholes, portals, and the knowledge that other forms can travel through these things, although, I am by far not the only person to know these things.

We have become much more open-minded at this time in history than at any known times in written history. Some are afraid of open-mindedness because it could begin to negate tradition. Although I feel tradition is a wonderful thing, I also believe there is so much more to the universe than we could even imagine. Didn't Einstein theorize imagination is more important than knowledge? I first heard that brilliant statement as a kid and it has stuck with me.

So, in widening our minds to the truth, we come forth in educating our brethren counterparts. I have long affected the ideals of man as one of constraint.

Carl taught me that we say to ourselves, that we mustn't stretch our minds to other ideas for the consequences would devalue our own existence, and so, we continue with long-held traditions that stunt our growth.

Depending on who we are in this world varies the knowledge of the conscience mind. Do we value ourselves on what we have or who we know? Sure, these are nice things. They do not lead us to the truth about ourselves in the universe, which is wide and whether we know it or not, we are part of a place, a place more far-reaching, and truly mind-blowing, with complexities we cannot even imagine.

In speaking about strategies for life, and if we have concluded by the last few paragraphs that we are indeed a wondrous race, a race of souls who are far more reaching than otherwise known, we can also conclude these are facts that have been limited in our previous knowledge, a knowledge that could bring about another amazing existence.

Our constraints have limited us to resources we could not

begin to imagine. In due course, I would say, you are of the mind to transgress previous beliefs, we can project these new ones in available use, simply saying, it is encouraging to know not all man is negated to hindrance. We value ourselves enough, to say, we contribute to society on a limited basis, however, I am open-minded to other possibilities.

When we begin to open ourselves to other thought-provoking ideas, we peel back layers of diseased thought processes.

If I could afford just one thought, I would say to all that if you feel uninspired then look in the mirror and say to yourself, and God, "If you will give me one drop of inspiration, I will follow through and give myself the pep talk and credit that I can well afford."

Inspiration is there; waiting to be tapped into. It doesn't have to take an act of God to remember it, for it is stored in the dark recesses of the mind.

Organized religion has taught us to keep certain things about ourselves at bay. What these religious cults teach us is to forget about who we truly are, and to put up a false front in reverence that in reality has no bearing.

The fruits of our labor sometimes come at a cost, a cost to the very person who we were meant to be, a non-judging ideal person of God. If we are truly part of God, then, we must look deep into ourselves to see that inner glow, that person who is waiting to be tapped into, that for whatever reason became someone who is true to everyone but themselves.

We can take a look at the open-minded person with awe, and we can say to ourselves, this person is truly a marvel because they can look at things from different points of view.

Our views can be skewed and even the best of us can become indifferent in the life school. The reason for this is that we aren't open-minded, however, what is our proof?

Our thought-provoking ideas can have an inkling of a point, but then we think to ourselves, is this idea one of clarity? Does it have something that is going to back it up? I will tell you all ideas have a source. They do come from somewhere, so where is this somewhere?

The open-minded person might think and say, I can't see it, I can't feel it, and I certainly can't touch it. I can sense it, though, I can sense that an idea is coming from a source I do not see, and maybe if you are a channel, you heard it. It was delivered to you from a voice you've heard before or a voice that is new to you. Is this voice wise, we ask ourselves, or will it lead us astray?

The voice of wisdom is easy to understand. It will not lead you astray. It will only challenge you and give you common sense advice that can only lead you to success. If we only learn to listen to that wise voice in our head, then know this, the sky is the limit.

POVERTY OF THE MIND

W HEN I SPEAK OF poverty of the mind, I am speaking about the lack of education in many countries, including our own, that focuses on things that can only be called surface education.

Surface education is what we begin in elementary school. Learning the three R's, reading, writing, and arithmetic. These are the lessons we need to begin our education life. Once we have these down, we can begin to move on to better lessons; however, are these lessons what we need to propel ourselves into the future?

I liken education as something to teach the norm. Is the norm going to be interested in geometry? Is the norm going to be interested in art, and so forth, and so on? Not everyone is of the mindset to make sense of calculus.

We each have our own way of learning. We are individuals and not the norm.

So, you see, when I speak of the norm, we are taught as the norm; however, from birth, we are as individual as the cells in our bodies. We come into our lives with a completely individual way of thinking, of creating, of feeling around in this great big world designed for the norm, and not for the individual, the free thinker.

These limitations in early education set us up for a life of drudgery, the mundane. Our instinct to be a free thinker is thrown out the door in the early years of our life. Education can start us to believe we are a number rather than the individual we were designed to be at birth.

Of course, there are always special situations that give certain people a leg up, to be a product of their imagination and not of normal societal thinking which we all feel is necessary in order to fit in with the mainstream.

If you feel the need to play the part of the individual free thinker, then you can do one of two things. You can start by allowing yourself to create who you want to be, and not who others have designated you to be. Second, I would give some thought to what makes you separate from others, and not the color of your eyes or hair. Do you like math? Do you see numbers in your head and find yourself calculating things in everyday life? Maybe you should go toward a career in accounting, or maybe, you can go further and build a career in physics.

Numerical values are found in everything we do, from banking, balancing our checkbook, and meeting a goal of designated hours of work, at the end of the day. Numbers have an infinite amount of ways they serve us in our lives, from dawn til dusk.

If we only knew about the numerical codes that do not present themselves directly in our daily lives, we would be mollified.

If we take a look at the cloud, this is where we get all our information from, when we compute at home, and at work. Everything we put into our computers goes into the cloud, the informational data we use every day.

Now think, what if a larger, more brilliant mass amount of information was out there, waiting to be tapped into by the free thinker, the individual who has decided to represent themselves instead of becoming part of the norm. This sparks the imagination for indeed science does not trivialize this information, this cosmic stream of data.

I find myself becoming more and more the individual thinker.

So many scientists have conducted experiments producing the knowledge of quantum waves, string theory, and more ideas that contain the numerical values, codes so to speak of data, data that can tell all our secrets of where we come from, and why we are here.

I highly suggest you go slow into this because the idea of this can become overwhelming.

If we seek this knowledge, we can find it by learning to take our brain waves into a deeper meditation, one that will bring about your knowledge, and pictures from another time and another place. It can show you the lives you've led, shocking the mind possibly into reminding you of not-always-pleasant memories. If you go this deep, it's okay, simply say to yourself, I am at this time and place, and I am safe. Don't allow yourself to be pulled into something long past.

This Akashic record of all things can also teach you; it can teach you about almost anything you want to learn about. Men and women from all different times in history have tapped into this numerical sequence of knowledge, and with the knowledge they have propelled themselves higher than they ever dreamed.

Knowledge is power. Knowledge can keep us from becoming the norm.

Poverty of the mind starts in youth and can contribute to what we process in our present life. We want to stay in this comfortable primitive brain. A brain that from youth served us in good times and bad times. When we try to move past the primitive brain, we find ourselves screaming, take me back to the safety of what I know. When the primitive brain gets us nowhere and keeps us stagnate, it keeps us away from long-desired goals and dreams.

So how do we get out of our primitive brain? How do we get away from this mindset that suited us until now? Instinct knows that there is more, more to life than what has grounded us and kept us going, whether it was comfortable or uncomfortable, it served us.

We can devise two ways to get out of this rut.

Stay true to your goals, and aim high. Change your way of thinking until it becomes as second nature as brushing your teeth or starting your coffee pot in the morning. The secret to changing your life starts with wanting those things so bad that have seemed out of reach for so long and prioritizing them until they become second nature.

Sounds easy, doesn't it.

Whether it is easy or not, depends on you, and to the reader of this book, if you cannot meet these goals alone, you can hire a coach of sorts and find someone who can guide you to success. It is not out of the limitations of your life, it is a possibility and to the positive thinker, you can stay the course and meet your goals.

What would that look like? What would it look like if you made more money? What if transforming yourself helped your family and friends? These are just a few things we can ask ourselves. The possibilities are endless if we give up this impoverished way of thinking and give in to the notion of succeeding.

THE LOGICAL THINKING MIND

I N SPEAKING ABOUT LOGICAL thinking, I am about to teach you that you can be open to other things without giving your honor up. Resist the urge to be a crowd thinker. A crowd thinker believes he will truly fit in if he thinks with the crowd. They fit in perfectly with other people who value themselves as the norm. If you stick with normal thinkers, you can become predictable, lacking a certain spice in your life. Nonetheless, we find ourselves comfortable in believing what everyone else believes because we fit that mold.

Now, think what it would be like to break free from the herd mentality, not that I'm saying there's anything wrong with it, just that you devalue a sense of self when you become part of the crowd who believe they are the right ones, and simply because giving up to long-held taught beliefs will set you up for ridicule by your so-called peers.

Religion has brainwashed its congregations for a very long time, not that everything about religion is wrong, it's just that religion can't begin to teach you everything about the truth, the truth you will be reminded of when you join the cemetery club.

Some people are more comfortable being sheep, part of the pack mentality, and if this is your way, by all means, don't give in to the hype. If you could, though, think for one minute, am I

16

being kept from knowledge of the universe, the universe I am a part of and have just forgotten for a brief moment in time?

I am not here to overanalyze, I am here to share what has been shared with me from my ancestors, the ancestors I am very familiar with on the other side, heaven or the fifth dimension, whichever you call it. For indeed, I am part of them, a loving group I have shared lives with, and who I share this genealogical strand that goes back thousands of years.

When I do meet them again, for I am looking forward to it, I shall be grateful for all they've shared with me in this life.

Most consider themselves logical thinkers, whether they are or not. The truth is many are illogical thinkers. This may seem confusing since I'm going to tell you the most brilliant use their illogical thinking. Aren't we all brilliant in our own way? Can we not think outside of the box? In terms of thinking outside of the box, we find ourselves going through mundane and things we trivialize. If we come across a problem, do we seek answers through already-known knowledge, or could it be we create new ways to find our answers? So, in understanding what I'm getting at is that we can collaborate with our logical and our illogical thinking, and if you find this confusing, then I will simply put it this way. Getting out of one's head offers us an opportunity to find new, if not different answers.

As an analyzer, I find myself questioning everything. I've asked the questions that have been history's mysteries for years. I simply like to understand it all. For a long time, I tried to think with the herd mentality because some far-thinking ideas I found too hard to believe, and even to understand, but some of the things in my early life could not be explained, so I began to revel in my illogical thinking.

Could it be that there is more than what religion and science can explain?

Albert Einstein delved into the illogical thinking. Do you think he pulled the theory of relativity out of his hat? Do you think Nikola Tesla dreamed up his idea of wireless energy and harnessing alternating current? Of course not. He revealed an outside source entered his consciousness, and this is how he came up with many of his inventions. What about Leonardo Da Vinci? He stared at a flickering candle and went into a meditative state, and this is how he said, he would come up with new ideas. Mathematician Srinivasa Ramanujan was one of the world's greatest mathematicians. He said complex equations were communicated to him in dreams, which was amazing in the fact that he grew up in India, and came from humble beginnings, and sometimes difficult conditions.

These free-thinking men used their genius in other ways, they tapped into that outer universal knowledge, knowledge that the ancestors have, and for some rare few who have the privilege to actually tap into.

This knowledge, if tapped into can bring about positive change, and as doubtful as this all sounds, could we possibly be on the verge of something remarkable, something to change the earth for the better? I know this idea of tapping into universal knowledge and law sounds rather impossible, however, if we remain quiet and try to raise our vibrational level, I believe all humans have the ability to do this. Some find it easier to do. It's the process of quieting our minds that can bring this about.

Practice this. It's really about learning to do meditation and taking your mind to a higher realm. You may begin to pick up thoughts, and at first, it may take a while to distinguish between your thoughts and the thoughts, which for many purposes could be your spirit guide. Yes, we all have them, and also, we have angels, and of course, our ancestors, all waiting to guide you on your journey.

For most, forget about making this transferred knowledge as a way to save the world, for that requires a mind that is very analytical, do this to learn about yourself and where you stand in this world. In time you will begin to see things from another perspective. The questions you ask, and the messages you receive, could be eye-opening, to say the least.

If you fall in the category of someone who bridges the gap of tradition, then you might be someone who is a true person of strategy. This may not resonate. It is, however, a truly divine way of being. For example, if you present yourself to the outside world as someone who is stagnate, and still you find ways to get things done, then you might be a person, who with a little training, can become a truly remarkable person.

The win game can be won. Aspire for greatness, forget the obstacles stopping you. Those old triggers will become just that, old triggers that are no longer a part of us. If we see ourselves in a much broader sense of who we are, we can begin to take the small steps to increase our power. We are powerful people where we come from, and connecting to your soul will bring increased chances of changing your life for the better.

Take our ancestors for example. Their traits were with them at birth. These genetic markers of a single individual person who can aspire to be who they want. We have every advantage to us that they did.

George Washington Carver was born into slavery and went on to become one of the most prominent inventors and scientists of his time. He had every obstacle stacked against him, however, his desire to learn made him one of the premier African Americans of the nineteenth century. He walked miles a day so he could get the education he desired.

It takes drive.

It takes an inner power in us to propel us to greatness. I would be remiss if I didn't mention the contributions this man-made. George Washington Carver was an agricultural scientist and inventor who developed hundreds of products using peanuts, sweet potatoes, and soybeans. Born at the end of slavery, Carver left home at a young age to pursue education, and would eventually earn a master's degree in agricultural science from Iowa State

Kristianne Ferrier

University. He would go on to teach and conduct research at Tuskegee University for decades.

He tapped into that drive at an early age. It does not matter what age we decide to become great, great within ourselves. We don't need to have the honors this man received for his contributions to agricultural science.

THE REVOLT OF THE MIND

A S WE BEGIN TO see ourselves from a new point of view, we can revolt against our old way of thinking. Of course, we don't need to go upon the rooftop and announce it for all to hear, we simply share it with our family and friends, who happen to be open to the idea. Maybe in time, you will begin to be drawn to like-minded people, there are people like us everywhere.

Now, like I said, announcing it may seem right in our exuberance, however, this kind of information does not gel with the mainstream. So, if you find yourself tapping into this highway of old news turned new, you may begin to have an inexplicable desire to go out and share with the rest of the world, however, as amazing as this all seems, others might see it as hogwash.

Remember, as I said, we all have a place in this world, and to tap into this knowledge brings you closer to what I like to call, the higher ascension. This is the beginning of the end for some. Once we begin to realize our place in the universe, we begin to see who we really are.

Some remarkable mediums, I have met, have mentioned they almost feel like they aren't part of this world, including myself. We have a higher esoteric vision.

Whether you are a taxi driver or you work on Wall Street, we all come from the same plane of existence. For when you realize this, you see you are no less, and no better. Many have led lives where their station is lower, and many have led lives in a higher station, nevertheless, we all come from the same form of being.

The chances in this current lifetime that you will become an open-minded thinker are rare, for there are few that will become instinctive enough to know the difference in this hierarchy of deliberate thinkers, however in saying this, I do devise a safe way of doing this. It's simply put, we can divide and conquer our truth into two separate categories.

These categories are not limited, but derivative of our ancestral knowledge. If we know about our inheritance from a different standpoint. This standpoint contains the knowledge of our true home, our true home of like-minded souls. For our journey seems long, however, in the scope of time it is very brief. We rehearse the variables to the knowledge that we contain in our DNA. Simply said, that is the ancestral knowledge we get from the lives lived before us. We contain our ancestors' traumas, their joys, and their pain.

To break these past life fractures, we must release them to the God energy. Say it in a prayer to yourself as you look into the light of the sun, "I no longer need the traumas of my lives, *including this one*. I'm giving them to God."

Forget the earth school, for it can be degrading to who we really are.

We shouldn't live in past lives, but we need to live in the ones we are in now.

The Hawaiians have a miracle healing prayer for peace, forgiveness, health, wealth, and happiness. Ho'oponopono prayers are incredibly powerful and are basically self-forgiveness and repentance prayers, but also reconciliation & cleansing prayers. Not only are they used to cleanse and heal anything, but they believe their prayers can help you obtain anything.

The Hawaiian Forgiveness Prayer is all about healing yourself, releasing your limitations and negativity, becoming free, and bringing you miracles too. Ask the Divine to help you forgive yourself for whatever is going on inside yourself that manifests as the problem.

The short four-phrase mantra and healing prayer for repentance, self-forgiveness & transmutation is simple. – *"I Love You, I am Sorry, Please Forgive Me, Thank You"*

What we fail to understand, we can be under siege of what our ancestors lived through. So, when we figure this out, we can retrieve certain aspects of this that are holding us back. Did our ancestor die on the battlefield of some long-forgotten battle. Do their earthly remains lie in a shallow grave of some farmer's field? Or like Teo, the Native American man whose remains are in a shallow grave outside my kitchen window. He was killed there in a battle over two hundred years ago and haunted our new house. Teo is finally at peace and has since taught me the medicine bowl.

What can happen is that our ancestor can be held back in their heavenly home by this circumstance, and what this can trigger, is a fracture to their soul, and that fracture can be passed down to us.

We need to understand with unlimited knowledge, that we could be here to deal with that pain, with that pain of our ancestor. To give it our thoughts and to reign it home. We can go to the source of the trauma, or we can simply go to our place of prayer or meditation and acknowledge the offense. Give it to the healing light of God. By representing our ancestor in this way, they can become whole again in their true home. In other words, even though they are at home in the heavenly realm, they can still be in unrest from this earthly trauma.

I have done this before, broken that human pain.

I have also helped family members on this side of existence.

The healing ceremony began with my going into meditation, where I connected to the ancestors. I could see them sitting at a long table. At the end was a king with an ancient-looking crown. I did not like his energy. It looked rather gray. I asked them to all unite and break these hundreds of years of traumas. Men in armor came forward with their swords raised and began to form a circle.

23

They lowered their blades with the tips to the ground and what I felt was inspired. The sentiment was all there and I can still feel the power of that moment. I knew what this represented. We are all united, united as one.

How powerful.

I could go into the reason for this ceremony, and it is an amazing story.

It's the long lost to time story of a prince, a descendant from several hundred years ago. It is a tragic love story, the love story of two that were married to others. John the Prince, had fallen in love with the beautiful Lady Cassandra, who was unfortunately married to a knight. They fell deeply and passionately in love; however, they could not be. The two had a couple of children together, including my ancestor.

The hierarchy frowned greatly upon this. She was taken in front of a tribunal of men, which was deeply mortifying to the lady, my ancestor. She was to give up her ways and to leave the prince alone.

My family member, who shall remain anonymous, was obsessed with studying this man, our ancestor, leading to the reason for this ceremony. In the end, it healed her and healed the soul who had been the prince, her soul mate.

She is no longer obsessed with her life as Lady Cassandra.

I also believe it healed fractures of other family members, including King Edward who had bad energy. I talked him into accepting his fractures, and he is now, from my knowledge living at peace on the other side.

And now, you know, there is a good chance, we lived as our own ancestor.

This same family member, who is also a writer, wrote a book about the story of a Native American family. She seemed very detailed in her knowledge, and this led me to wonder, as an author, we write what we know.

I asked the ancestors, and they began to tell the story.

24

This is also a love story from a German side. Michael Myers was a soldier during the American Revolution and settled in Kentucky with his German wife, Margaret, where they had several children. In the late 1700s, Michael, an engineer by trade, went with a surveying team into the upper northeast around Lake Michigan. While there he met an Ojibwa and French-Canadian woman, named Forest Woman.

He was away from home and probably lonely and he fell in love with her. She had a son with Michael, my third-great-grandfather, also called Michael. It was decided she would raise him until he was old enough to travel. Five years later he went back to retrieve his son, which was devastating to Forrest Woman, and she grieved greatly. She was brave, brave enough to give up the son she so loved in order for him to have a better life.

These lives resonate with me. They are a part of me. Their sacrifices were great, however, these ancestors kept going. From records, Michael Myers II led a sometimes difficult life. He had an education and fought in the Mexican-American War. His daughter's mantle clock is in my dining area.

I would be remiss if I didn't mention that in order to give a hundred percent, we sometimes have to give up things we love in order to move ahead. This makes us stronger. Remember the adage, what doesn't kill us, makes us stronger.

We've all lived lives, lives that have left us tattered and torn.

More on fractures later.

THE FORGOTTEN MIND

W E ALL STRUGGLE IN our lives on earth. Each one of us gives up our divine light in order to bring higher knowledge, so when a soul struggles, he must find his way by giving into his truth for he is divine, and he only can know what his truth represents, so in doing this he must conquer his fear, and when his fear gives way to true knowledge it will lead this lost soul to his true salvation.

What do you get from this? We give up our divine light to gain higher knowledge. I wrote this as a way to invite the reader to analyze themselves. We come here to learn, to give way to fear, to understand what life means to us.

We give up our divine life many times to learn.

What if you found out you are a reincarnation of your uncle, or perhaps your fourth great-grandmother? These things have happened in my family.

In Christianity, we are taught not to believe in reincarnation. Many of the world's religions believe that our souls move from one body to another.

I have long held a fascination with reincarnation, and maybe that is why I first remembered my last life during the 1920s. Probably fifteen years ago, I had a vivid dream. In a dream, I saw a picture of a beautiful young dark-haired lady in an oval frame that resonated with me. She had beads in her hair and looked like a flapper. The pages of an old photo album opened and these people stepped out of the pictures and told their story. Over the years I've remembered my last life as a young woman named Lillian Elizabeth Baker, Lilybeth to her parents. I did know she died of tuberculosis in her middle twenties. I can't explain how I remember past lives any more than I can explain my abilities as a medium.

Visiting Waverly Sanitorium in Louisville Kentucky brought it back.

Recently, inside the now ruins of the old hospital, I looked down the long hallway downstairs and had a strong reaction. The place is very haunted, and I assumed I was picking up on spirit energy. Upstairs, on the top floor, I felt the soul of a distraught nurse who had been found hanging back in the day. I stood in the area where she had supposedly been found, and where I heard her lamented cry, "That man brutalized me." She also said he was not the man everyone thought he was. I tuned into the story. He had been a doctor, and she had been a nurse, and I think a flirtation he took too far. The doctor had physically assaulted her and she became pregnant. She threatened to tell, and not wanting his reputation ruined, or his wife to find out, he chose to end her life.

I used psychology to get through to her. It was not her fault, and she needed to move on because being in that state of anger did her no good. She told me she would probably eventually move on, and I think she was scared being pregnant out of wedlock would be judged in heaven.

Of course, this is poppycock. Religion is a wonderful thing, but it can also be destructive when it teaches us to be fearful and can trap us in a living hell of our own making. My guide told me she moved on not long after I talked to her.

After I returned home that place continued to haunt me for the next couple of days. I began to have memories of that long hallway. I could see a pristine hospital with lots of nurses in white. The walls were painted, not the building that is in ruins today. I remembered being there towards the end of my

27

then life. Lillian had been there. The sanitorium was not safe, especially for women. I remembered she had been assaulted by a male patient, and then moved to a sanitorium closer to home, where she used means to end her pain. Over the years, I have remembered bits and pieces of her life. She was part Italian, from Chicago, and from a broken family. She married young in the nineteen twenties and left for Las Vegas, She became a showgirl to make her living, and her husband held mobster ties in the 'outfit.' Partying and drinking and surrounding herself with bad people and her husband's disregard led to her contracting TB.

This all came out and I felt her grief, her part of me that had infected my now life.

Lily came from a well-to-do family but had been let down by her parent's divorce, and her father's tyranny. She'd had such promise. My guides and ancestors supported me through the next few days. And one morning, I heard my new friend, Thunder Cloud, whom I had helped guide to the other side at the old Fort Knox.

"Meo ho, my friend," he greeted. He told me in his voice full of wisdom, "Each life is not meant to hamper us, it's meant to help us grow." He asked me, "How did that life make you grow?"

I thought long and hard. I recalled her beauty and adventurous nature. She may have been young and naïve, but she did live life to the fullest. And maybe it did teach me to surround myself with a better quality of people.

Family members have told me over the years they also remembered parts of past lives.

My father remembered being in a past life as a World War I flying ace, and my son remembers a life as a young German soldier, named Hans, in that same war. An aunt has the strong feeling of being an Irish nun, and my sister remembers an English life where her husband threw her in a hole to die during the Middle Ages.

I do see the humor in all of this, believe it or not, the other side has a great sense of humor. My fifteenth great-grandfather is very humorous. I refer to them as, Grandpa 'Hot Spur' Percy, only because he was given this moniker for his remarkable horsemanship. Lord Henry Percy, his real name, unfortunately, was killed, drawn, and quartered at the battle of Shrewsbury over six hundred years ago. He's since been my brother-in-law, George, and my grandson, William Henry, and he is also one of my three main guides.

My main spirit guide, William, also George's brother in my life as William's wife Catherine, has a terrific sense of humor and keeps me laughing. Now if I've confused you, I'm sorry. Can you imagine what it's like to find out you and your sister were each other's grandmothers several generations back, and your son was your third great-grandfather? It can make your head spin. The ancestors have a way of keeping us on our toes.

Now, to continue with the ancestors, we can find a sense of pride in realizing these remarkable people who came before us. They led the way, the charge, so to speak, and we are here to pick up the pieces where they left off.

It elevates the spirit to know how far we've come. Each individual person from our family tree has contributed to our being here by a fluke of surviving the earth school, contributing to it through wars, floods, through all sorts of lives, religions, colors, and nationalities, ending with us, the new generation. Can it get better than that, I suspect not for I am an individual in my own right.

We produce circumstances in each of our lives, some good, some bad, some mediocre, and some like Grandpa Hot Spur, who I can envision blonde, tall, and good-looking, on his white steed charging into battle with his rebel group to fight against their tyrannical king. Lord Henry is written on the walls of history, and also Wikipedia where you don't have to look too hard to find him. That's the way our families are, we go through lives intended for good, we make mistakes, we make history, and if we have courage enough, someday, somebody, might write a story about your escapades, as writers have for some of my ancestors.

If we agree to disagree, we might find some common balance. These stories, for the most part, have been lost to time, and are challenged by the most hardened genealogists. I've had more than one look at me and say, "Are you sure, everyone wants to be related to someone famous."

Well now, I cannot exactly say to them, "Um, well, I do know, because they told me so."

They would laugh me out of the room and throw me out on my ear.

And you, as the reader knows what this means, I have to do the hard work, the fun-loving work of searching through old moldy tomes, scouring hours on the computer, or spending a million dollars and just breaking down and hiring a freakin professional genealogist. I love research, however, sometimes it's disheartening when you find no answers, only to have Grandpa William or Grandmother Sarah say in your ear, "You're going to have to go to the Library of Congress, that's the only place you will find these records." Have you ever looked at the Library of Congress's website? Here's where I insert that crazed-looking emoji with its tongue hanging out of its mouth. I think I will get that root canal instead.

Earlier today, my fifth Great-Grandfather, Colonel Richard, and my father-in-law in that life said to me, "You've found the answers you need. You are one of us."

As wonderful as this is, many family members over the last hundred years have been trying to make the connections for the proper pedigrees, so with my brief moment in this last life, I want to set the records straight for the next generations, and if I have to go to the Library of Congress to do it, so be it. By the way, Lt. Colonel Richard helped write the Kentucky constitution and was one of George Washington's officers, not that it makes me all that.

THE MIND OF THE
SOUL RESCUER

I CONSIDER THIS CHAPTER TO be the most important. The reason for writing this book.

I did not know why I felt such a need to help others go into the light, sending them back to their true home. I just knew that if I was in their shoes, I would want someone to help me.

Being a medium, I've learned there is a realm of spirits. They can come from far away, and I refer to them as the wandering ghosts. As a medium, occasionally, these souls see my light and come into my home, my sanctuary.

These ghosts taking up space in my home can cause an energy drain on the person they direct their energy to. I've been made accustomed to these not-trivial ghosts who visit and seek solace, or to just have someone to direct their negative emotions at for the lack of a better word.

Remembering they are a person without a body is imperative because the ire it brings out in me, to be the sought out as a source for giving these emotions they gained in the earth school. Depression, anxiety, rage, and fury, to name a few.

So, in gaining the upper hand in these futile attempts to bring me down to their levels, I must stay grounded, and I must keep sharp in mind that, with help from the other side, I can bring these souls back to solace and peace. By staying balanced in your own physical and mental state, you can keep from being drained by these poor lost souls.

The very essence of these ghosts remains hidden, and they just need to be reminded of their divine selves.

Curiosity keeps me wondering how these souls got into this lost realm of the ghost world. I have spoken to some and learned their stories, of course, and there is a wide variety of reasons they missed the opportunity at their death to seek the light. Many are suicides, which leads me to understand more about the trauma of the Earth School.

Spirits like Clementine Fowler, a lady from the 19th century. She's since come to me and regarded my work with the spirits.

Recently, my family and I traveled to Miami and got on the cruise ship, *Harmony of the Seas*. On board, we met some amazing people. A young woman from the Philippians courageously making her living as a maître de far away from her young son and husband. Lourdes waited on us every evening in the dining room of the ship. She inspired me with the care and love my family received every evening. She and Paul, the man who filled our drinks and brought bread to our table, became part of our family for a week and shared in our off-the-wall humor. Jeff, the accountant from Los Angeles, whom we tended to run into on beautiful Caribbean beaches, lived life to the fullest and also inspired me with his infectious positivity and deep knowledge.

These people are in your life for a brief moment in time and feel like long-lost friends. Another person I met on this trip, was a young woman named Amanda. I met her in awful traffic. My son, who is finding his way as a medium also, said he sensed a heavy presence. I closed my eyes and connected with a beautiful blue-eyed blonde. I could see her clearly in my mind's eye. She lamented, *"If only I hadn't gone to Tallahassee that day."*

Amanda showed me a mental image of her wedding not long before the *accident*. I kept hearing the name Julie and the story came out. She and Julie traveled on that unfortunate day leading to their untimely deaths. I could see Amanda reach down to probably the radio knob, and look up too late. While Julie had moved on, Amanda stayed put on that busy long strip of interstate highway, trying to warn other drivers not to take their eyes off the road. With some prompting, Amanda eventually went into the light.

She came to me as I wrote this, to say, "I understand now it was an accident, and I did not mean to kill my friend."

It was an unfortunate judgment call leading to the crash. I won't forget Amanda and her story, and I am so glad she moved on.

Someday, I suspect, hopefully, I will meet some of these incredible souls I've aided in moving on, and whose stories have touched me.

If you take a channel like me, and you listen, you might learn what these spirits are about. None remembers their divine selves, or they would not be trapped in a lost world. They seek the answers from mediums because they are the only humans who can hear them, and if you respond to them, they are more likely to focus all that energy on you.

What if we took an actual look at these souls and understood why they have either chosen or for some reason or another, found themselves trapped in this sort of purgatory existence? In seeking you out, they hope you will know the answer to how to get them out of this isolated, and many times dreadful state of mind.

I warrant you this, if it were you in their shoes, you would seek the same salvation.

Now, on how to aid them, this influx of ghosts seeking retribution. You must put their minds at ease and explain they are out of touch with that divine reality they actually belong to. If you give them a chance, most are probably more confused than evil, and yes, they can be annoying. Given a chance, most take my advice to give their earth traumas to God, and then they go willingly with the archangels who deliver them safely home.

My advice is to be very careful if you open that door yourself because doing so could allow other entities to come in. I feel much safer asking the archangels to give them safe passage.

The door, a portal, which transports us back and forth to home and earth, in my mind's eye is a swirl of energy, and at the top is a horizontal rectangle door, and once they go through, I've heard thank you, which humbles me. It could be two or three, other times seven or more.

Some of these ghosts have been rule breakers, the people some might call the dregs of society, the contemptible souls who lived for themselves, or lived a life of depravity, or never just got what life was about. The rare negative ones, or non-human. These are removed with sage, and also Christian prayers.

Please be sure to tell them to give their earth trauma to God when they go.

Anyway, the human spirits who are not so nice and say untoward things can be some of the worst, serial killers even, and I will not condone their actions. They are treated accordingly when I call on my angel who whisks them away This magnificent angel, believe it or not, is St. Michael. I thank God for him and his fellow archangels and value everything they do for me. If a spirit is a pest, I simply call on this avenging angel or his comrades, and they escort them home.

If I could make myself clearer, I couldn't, do not allow yourself to be bombarded by these souls bent on destruction because that is what they knew in the life they last lived on earth, and how to go about this is much easier than can be imagined. A dose of their own medicine for being a pest and not leaving. If you have not developed a thick skin or devised a way to shut them out, then simply do this, give them the old heave hoe calling in the angels. An undeveloped medium, especially the young, can have issues with being bombarded by these invisible pests. Create a barrier around you, and stand your ground.

Of course, if you are a medium who is not well grounded, and have emotional issues from youth or lack of experience, then hold onto your hats here. You need to strengthen who you are. You must become an evolved person who knows who you are, and who has figured out how to win at this game called life.

Seek out a counselor or life coach, learn how to be a problem solver, and don't take flak from these lost humans bent on destroying you.

One such negative spirit came around me, and I warned him to back off his negative talk, and he finally came around to speak to me civilly. He and a few other souls were guided by St. Michael hastily home, faster than the speed of light.

A short time later, he came back to tell me he had not been walled up in a stadium, as had been divulged by the press. This spirit was none other than the Teamster Boss, Jimmy Hoffa, and he wanted to tell his story.

Jimmy told me his body had been dumped along the route of the Statin Island Ferry the night he disappeared. "I went to a meeting," he told me, "And was jumped by a couple of goons. Enforcers of the mob. They strong-armed me and told me to get the money I owed them, and I told them they could go to hell. One back-handed slap told me they meant business, and if I didn't do what I was told, I figured I would be killed. Anyway, one thing led to another, I didn't have the money and the two goons shot me right through the heart. After that I found myself in this purgatory existence, until I got wind there was a lady who could probably help, and that was you."

I had to laugh, and not because of this man's horrendous death and body being dumped in the New York harbor, only because I never know who I will entertain when it comes to souls seeking redemption.

He continued saying, "When all of this went down, I was incredulous at how far the mob would take this. I figured they would rather give me time to pay it back, rather than kill me and never receive a cent. This was a message to all who go against mob rules, you can't win, so be prepared. I never wanted my life to end this way, although it gave me notoriety. It ended way too soon and I didn't get to see my children's futures and witness the births of grandchildren. If I could do it all again, I never would have taken a chance and gotten tangled with the mob. Notoriety isn't all that it is cracked up to be."

One of the histories' mysteries solved, if you believe.

I learned from him what the ghost world is like.

It isn't just a fog; it is like a dream that never ends. You feel like your body is in some suspension-type existence and you never wake up from this dream.

Jimmy wanted me to understand and told me that when I feel like I am being robbed of my daily life because of these needy spirits, to please remember what I do is a kindness they can never repay, and if he could give you all the money in the world for what I'd done for him, he would in a heartbeat. He humbled me.

The importance of soul recusing is the other side wants their loved ones back. Can you imagine your soulmate waiting for hundreds of years for you to come out of this reverie of the ghost world? It can be excruciating.

The reason souls gather around my house is because they see the light of two mediums living under the same roof. The ghosts have told me there is knowledge of what I do in their realm. For everyone who has this light, please dim the third eye, because you are more than likely drawing spirits. It is the *kindest* thing you can ever do for the other side to send them home. The ancestors have told me there is a deep need for people with these abilities to help the ghost world. You may have to be a psychologist for these spirits, after all, they are still humans without a body.

And yes, this can be intimidating at first. It is not for the faint of heart because you might draw negative human spirits, however, I have learned the hard way, and as I said, there are safe procedures, and in that, I am still learning.

I did learn where the portal is in my house, and I do believe I closed it permanently.

I am told by the ancestors that in doing this for ghosts, your soul will be elevated in our heavenly home, and as I said, I am doing this to help and not for any attention I might receive or, I had to laugh, as I told my guide, I need no ticker tape parade.

TIME CONTINUUM
AND THE MIND

C OMING BACK TO SPEAKING to the ancestors, if we give this idea a chance, and we ourselves decide to look for a new way of seeing the world, I can give you two ideas.

The idea comes from the Theory of Relativity. You have two interreacting laws, special relativity explains the absence of gravity, and general relativity explains the evolution of time. This idea weighs heavy on some because it doesn't free them of the actual concept of time. Now if you could think, I am part of a much bigger place, a place that doesn't have time constraints, we might begin to see that we belong to a much bigger universe. A universe that is bigger than any of us can imagine.

You can project your ideas to a higher platform, a platform that gives us a reachable goal.

For now, think about the times you spent with grandparents, and family members who are now long gone. These family members were important to you at the age of development, and in some instances, we feel they are still part of our lives, only in a different place. Where is that place? We are taught in religion this place is called heaven. So, where is heaven? Do we look to the sky? If we seek answers to this, then we can alleviate the idea heaven is in the sky.

This leads to one answer, Heaven must be in a dimension,

and you can get there through a portal. So, now we ask, where are these portals, how can I find them?

Well, this answer is simple, these portals are all around us. If our mind can now go to the science part of the equation. A portal you ask? Scientists call them black holes, which is a larger one, and then the smaller ones are called wormholes. A portal is simply the vehicle in which you travel through dimensions. Dimensions you ask? Yes, this can all be explained.

A portal is a vortex of energy that can project us to our heavenly souls' home. When the time comes, this light, this vortex of energy will appear to you and deliver you home. This energy transports us from heaven to earth, and is faster than the speed of light.

We can barely wrap our heads around this idea, that we are actually light beings. These incredible beings, who flourish on earth for a moment, and then we are transported home for all purposes.

In a way, isn't this part of what we are taught in religion?

If we look at the fundamentals of religion, we see that it lacks the teaching of the more science-related answers. The answers we seek to what we are doing here, and where we come from, because surely these incredible brains of ours don't just die out.

In knowing this, we start to see a new transformation in ourselves, and this transformation can lead us to more questions if our inquiring mind seeks to know more answers.

Here's a clue. Why not begin to look at things as if they aren't just static? We are higher vibrationally than we can even imagine. The level of magneticity in our whole bodily structure is explained by neutrons and molecules. Our molecular structure is a far more advanced system than we could ever realize. In our menial day-to-day activities, we do not begin to understand the fantastic individuals we are. If we had one iota of this, we would be mollified.

In getting back to how we can get in touch with our ancestor, I'll again devise two ways.

This structure of ours is designed to do many things. These brains of ours can think up capacities we don't even acknowledge. Our bodies are designed to move and propel us through our daily chores. What if our brains could generate new thoughts, thoughts that do not come from us? Thoughts that come from outside our own thinking. I merely suggest that we try and listen, listen for those thoughts that are not our own.

Maybe your grandmother died many years ago, and for some reason, your thoughts go to her. This thought is not just a memory, but a very strong feeling of her. Could it be she is with you at that moment? Visiting from her heavenly realm.

This is possible, and many have felt this from time to time. A strong feeling of a long-lost relative that is more than just a feeling. This is a visitation. Not a ghost. This is a time that you could try and communicate. Close your eyes and allow your thoughts to go to her.

You may receive a message, a message of love. A message of I'm still here. That relationship still has value. You don't ever lose the ones you love. They simply are in another place you cannot even begin to imagine. And those bonds never break. You will see them again soon. Sooner than you know.

To many, this is comforting. You never lose the ones you love. They have just gone into the light, through the portal, and back to all of everyone's true home.

So now, imagine the energy it requires to propel through this vortex of time. Yes, time is limited on Earth, so when we think about time and space, we can't begin to understand the nonexistence of time on the other side. We have been limiting ourselves by always thinking about time. On the other side, we aren't on a time schedule that pressures us to not be late for work, make sure we pick up our children on time, and not miss out on those important meetings. We aren't pressured where we come from.

That sounds rather wonderful, or again maybe, this could be rather boring.

Now back to the idea of not being consumed by time. What would this feel like? At the moment, it might sound pretty good. Especially when you have to get Timmy to his ball game, and then come home fix supper, and then pick him up, oh, and don't forget the laundry, and then just think, tomorrow you have to do this all over again.

Heaven sounds pretty good, doesn't it?

Now, what if you thought about the eons of unlimited time that you live in heavenly bliss? For the great minds on the other side that would feel like they needed more. Wouldn't you want to get away from the mundane, the dreadful cycle of bliss? Of course, there are moments on earth, when we strongly feel that sounds wonderful.

Well, to many, we just need more. We want to expand our brains, our knowledge of other things. Things we cannot know about on the other side.

This is where it begins. It starts with an idea, an idea of a life. A brief vacation from the dreaded heavenly mundane. This is where we start to come up with the vision of a life on earth that will teach us new information and lead us on new adventures.

Could it be? Our life is an adventure, away from a place that is so wonderful, that we feel the need to get away from it for a while. Wow, that's a new look at our life, that it could actually be an adventure. Then what are we doing with our lives, are we simply going through the day-to-day activities, making breakfast, making lunch? What if we saw ourselves from a new perspective, then? Our lives might now seem exciting.

With this new perspective, what could we do? I don't mean take up skydiving or some other adrenaline junky activity, but to look at our lives with value. Value the time we have left on earth, for when we get home, and some time has passed, we might say, well, I think it's time for another adventure.

Fifty lifetimes on Earth are enough for me, and I am now retiring from the earth school. I've learned enough, I'm sure.

If we think we want to seek more adventure, more time spent learning, whatever you desire, then think to yourself, I want to be a person, a person I can be proud of, who is not afraid to live their best life, to speak their truths because if we undulate ourselves to a lackluster existence, we forget the big picture.

We are designed to give one hundred percent, even though, we may only give eighty-five percent. If we regulate our daily work life by numbers, numbers that show how many contributions you laid out during the day. And why would we give a numerical value to our daily grind? It is because we exist to fill numbers and not value, as an example, productivity equals a certain quota, we exist to be productive from the hours of 9 to 5.

Quantity instead of quality.

Regarding this, I will give you an example. Figures are fleeting. One times one is one.

Well, the truth is, this is a quantum figure, a figure that is designed to give us an ideal, an ideal of the time spectrum. A novice idea of the time continuum. All of us are taught basic math in school. We aren't taught the logic behind math; beyond the numerical values we hold in our minds. These values are important to us and to our civilization. In order to live in a prosperous world, we must use numerical calculations in order to have productive lives.

This all may sound to the average thinker as trivial, however, I can assure you, that we are a civilization of intricate thinkers who need math to produce world order.

For the genius mind, the mind that makes sense of calculus and geometry, if we go to these mathematical formulas for our main stays, then we will find the unequivocal actions that prove we are superhuman, a race of thinkers who justify what we see as logic.

Reasoning, as it may, is for the advanced mind to see. How can we tap into this for ourselves? Have we ever desired to be superhuman, to have knowledge that propels us forward, then I can say if you only have the desire, you can receive this information, as it were. We reproduce equations to fit ideals in our charts, our charts that are filled with the data we need to finish these lives we designed to send us forth.

Our lives are figured into such thought-provoking numerical values, values that can bring a sense of judgment we bring into these existences. This may seem like trivial bunk to some, it is, however, the essence of who we truly are in this universe.

Our time here on earth is rational if we only look at certain stats, stats that are in our charts that have turned us into the person we are today. And not just a trivial person, however, a super-minded person who can run rings around the early nomads.

At this time in history, we have become far more advanced than in known historic civilizations. We calculate, we divide, and we make numerical calculations not previously known. We have become a civilization of productive citizens on the world stage who will no doubt lead to the destruction of the population of this world, and how you ask?

We've become so advanced in science, we have produced weapons of mass destruction to strong-arm other countries into staying in their territories, however, as we know, these weapons put into the hands of an aggressor, an aggressor of inhumanity, who takes lightly the lives of their own people, as well as others in civilized nations.

We have become so well advanced which will inevitably lead to the annihilation of many people on Earth, as well as animals, and the health of Mother Earth.

Our ancestors fought against such aggressors to the point they had to build a weapon of mass destruction to stop the infiltrations of mad men, who in their insanity, desired to take over the world. At this moment in time, these weapons are in the hands of greedy and ambiguous men, who in their warped minds can only see the idea of bigger and better things for themselves and not see that this earth was designed for all.

What does this statement trigger for you? Does it bring you to revulsion? It should be because if it weren't for monstrous leaders in this world, we would have the freedom to be who we desire, a group of free-living people, who have no fear of these despicable humans.

As tragic as this all sounds, I would like to turn this around to a positive. A way of looking at the world with new lenses. We may reproduce into our lives new ways of thinking, for if we devise a new pattern of thinking, then surely, we will see our lives as prosperous. If we devise a plan to become the engineer of our life, so to speak, we become the lead in our own show.

I have found in my own life many ways to change things for the better. If we evaluate the properties of our life and separate the trivial from the things that hold us back, then we will begin to see a new you. This new you, what would this look like? A Freudian term would be, for example, we limit ourselves to the time we spend spinning our wheels. What does this statement mean to you? It means we spend so much time trying to get to where we want to be in our lives, we forget the processes it takes to get us there, and what can occur is we never quite get to the point we desire to achieve. So, in saying this, we must take a stronger hold of our own legacy, a legacy for all purposes, we will cede to our children.

Do we want them to have a remembrance of us as not being the accomplished person we could have been? Someone who frittered their life away with no consequences. That is the legacy that many have left behind.

It's true, that we will all lead the life we want to, however, if we hold no accountability in our life, surely, we will fail to see the person we could have been. Many have raced through life not seeing the value of it because we have allowed our primitive brain to take hold, and we have not gotten in touch with that person we were at birth, a new human, from a soul that saw a life of value at the time they were conceived.

So, my point is, what do you want your legacy to be?

I have spoken to many of my ancestors and found that they are proud of the woman I've become. Now, being the humble person I am, I appreciate their compliments, it is them that I thank because of their legacies, their trials and errors made me who I am, for without them, I am not me. So, in saying this, we must carefully analyze the person we are, for our children are watching and learning from us, and what they learn could be passed down to a wonderful existence on this planet called Earth.

A MIND OF DIVINE
KNOWLEDGE

I N SPEAKING ABOUT DIVINE knowledge, I've devised a way to
make it understandable.

Never underestimate the value you have as an individual.
This knowledge we seek is indivisible. We seek the knowledge of
the ages. Seek ye through the ages, for we are profound within
ourselves.

These sentences seem so powerful. It makes you think.
Could it be we are more than what we realize? This idea could
transform your thinking, I am more than a mere human being.
These magnificent thoughts come from out of the blue from time
to time. Things like, thoughts create patterns in life. You are
unique in your own way. Remember, life has many roads; which
one will you take?

Where did these thoughts come from? Somewhere outside
of myself? A place I wanted to know about, to understand. If we
can be given this knowledge from a higher place, then I certainly
want to know about it.

Over the years, I began to adjust my way of thinking. I gave
much consideration to the lessons I was learning. I am by no
means a devout Christian; however, Christianity has had a place
in my life. I don't normally go to church. I find church sometimes
demeaning to my way of thinking. I don't mean this in a severe
way, or a critical way. It just didn't resonate with me.

These dull stories told year after year. We go through the whole church year. We start the new year with the epiphany, leading us to lent, the whole sad remembrance of Easter and what it stands for. And then the long stretch of Pentecost, leading eventually to Advent and back again to Christmas, during which many agnostics and non-believers have regulated the holiday to Santa Claus.

So, in looking at Christianity, for many it has become dull, a retelling of stories, which may have some truth to them, but also simply parables written thousands of years ago by some long-gray-haired old man.

We can have faith that Jesus was a real person on earth and that he did indeed have special gifts. That we can be certain. Whether he turned water into wine is debatable. Could he have simply had the ability to be a powerful magician? The thought is sacrilegious to some.

Now, like I said, the bible was written thousands of years ago, two thousand to be more exact. Shouldn't we analyze this? Something written that long ago. Could it be that the bible's words have been contaminated? Could the bible's translation have been disturbed from its actual meaning? It has been said that the early Roman Catholic church was led by men who wanted Jesus Christ to be pure, this man who was non-sexual and presented with a squeaky-clean image.

What rot I tell you; he was a man of great moral character, I assure you. However, he was man of marriageable age. Some have questioned Mary Magdalene's place in his life. Could she have possibly been his wife, the mother of his children?

Now, I understand this goes against everything we are taught in the church. Let's go back to the early Catholic church. Could it be that she was devalued to a whore for the sake of Christ's purity? Well, I won't say for sure, however, it will give you something to think about.

The words of Jesus Christ told the truth. We must peruse

through the statements he made. He said there is everlasting life and that if we live a life of good honest deeds, then we will find a place in heaven.

Now, back to the ancestors. These stories handed down.

I do know as a genealogist that many of my family's records have been contaminated, and this has been in only the last one-hundred and fifty years. Wrong spellings, etc.

One record suggests several more children than there actually were. I think the researcher mixed up the next generation with the last generation. We are all fallible, fallible to human mistakes. If we just want answers badly enough, we might just create them.

In my records, which are available for public access, I have typed in a few of those answers given to me by my ancestors. I trust them more than I trust some distant cousin who did some sloppy research.

Well, enough of that.

We can all regulate ourselves with the knowledge, we are human.

I have long considered, that we are all divine, there's a spark of genius in all of us. So, now what if we tapped into that knowledge, that knowledge of the Akashic records?

Now some of you may be aware of the Akashic records. I won't go into the long boring story of them, because that would be the longest book ever written.

Just imagine for a minute, a far-reaching library that stretches the whole extent of time and space, as far-reaching as the eye can see. This vast wealth of information that stores every piece of knowledge that has ever existed.

If we tap into it, we just might find the answers we are looking for. If you can imagine such a fantastical amount of information that could send us on the path we seek. I can say I have not tapped into these records. If I seek knowledge, I simply ask my ancestors and they are more than happy to give me the answers to the questions I want to know, although, it wouldn't hurt for me to try to tap into the Akashic records, just once.

Well, now maybe you as the reader have concluded, that we are more than we seem, and with this new information, maybe we could conquer the world, or maybe just live a much fuller life.

As I said before, there is no reason to go out and try extreme sports, however, maybe this could lead to a new spark, a spark of the imagination, if Einstein really did believe imagination is more important than knowledge, then we can start to become more aware of our frontal lobe and where it leads us.

By tuning into what is around us, in the esoteric world, we might learn secrets of some long-lost world, or the secrets of the world around us now. As logical thinkers, we tend to want to believe what is right in front of us. Now the illogical thinker will begin to see things in a new way. Ask yourself, what if what I see in front of me is not everything there is?

Could it be there is a vast universe of knowledge just waiting for you to devour, and that we can seek knowledge of more than what the gray matter of the brain can bring about?

If we begin to expand our knowledge, we can begin to be more objective, and more literal to the extent of examining our forefathers' legacies. In them, we find ourselves. Were they broad-minded in life? Did they contribute to life in a way of making it better for others?

Well, in understanding what they stood for, you can see that we may agree with how they conducted their lives, or we may disagree, it's only in the way we see them that we may begin to see ourselves. Were they selfish? You may be the most giving person in the world; however, you still have the same DNA lineage that they carried. Our lineage carries traits. They may have been blonde and blue-eyed, while you are brown-haired and brown-eyed. This does not matter.

We are the next generation leading the pack.

So, why is this all important?

It has more hidden meanings than we can understand. This value of our ancestors. They were more than just a person who lived, for if they hadn't lived the life they lived, we would not be here. Our understanding of them may be hidden in records, there may be old pictures of them on the wall of your living room.

We are given this heritage as a reminder that all is not static.

Wisdom does come from within. We find when we become in tune with that part of ourselves, that inner knowledge waiting to be tapped into. Our inner voice can become our guide map, the map to that information about ourselves that can make us thrive.

We are born with this wealth of truth, this genetic truth that we are born into a world with already sequences of data, of DNA. Our DNA tells us about those that came before us, with traits that will tell you inherited your grandmother's height, that you inherited your great-grandfather's green eyes. In these DNA structures, you can find wisdom and this wisdom will tell you about yourself. If you are predisposed to crave certain foods, if you rely on yourself and not others, simple things that seemingly have no real meaning other than you just see these quirks as just patterns of your personality.

No one is quite like you. You are one of a kind. I liken this to viewing ourselves as a whole person of a percentage of different genes you were given at birth. Kind of like if you look at a pie chart, a family tree that keeps growing and growing. Imagine a tree whose branches go wider than the naked eye can see.

Now back to the part of genetic sequence data. Our data can tell us much. It eternalizes the truth of who you are. If you wish to be a certain type of person, then you can learn about yourself from this data, and figure out what you need to do to become this person, the person you've always dreamed of becoming. If you are the type of person who believes dreams can come true, then you will have a much easier time figuring this out.

Imagine you are on a tropical island with your back against a palm tree and visually you are looking up at the blue puffy cloud sky. In your auditory sense, you can hear the waves lapping against the beach. Your nose tells you about that scent of the fragrant ocean, that smell of the beach, while you spread your fingers in the sand, feeling that powder of refined sea shells. With your tongue, you taste the salt water that fills the air.

You have now used all five senses. Now still in that state of awareness, try to close your eyes and connect with that unseen wisdom, that part of you which has been there since birth. Feel the tranquility that surrounds you. You are connecting with your higher self. You are evolving into a person who is not only in touch with all five senses, you are now connecting with a part of yourself you only dreamed about.

As you breathe in deeply, you ask yourself, what is it that I need to become whole, to become that person from birth who was already designed to be that person I want?

We feel things in our lives, things that sometimes we question. Do I really feel the way I am supposed to feel? This may seem a little illogical. Shouldn't we understand ourselves, our place in this world?

We tend to be creatures of habit, as I've said before. We rise and shine and fill our days with the same tasks, tasks that must be done to keep balance within our lives. Are we too complacent? Do we dare get off our track, so to speak? Do we deviate from patterns we've created? Of course not, for without balance in our lives, we could become topsy-turvy, and that would not be good for anyone in our familiar circle.

So, if we decide to connect with our genetic wisdom then we must take the time to do the fact-checking of integrating that hidden part of who we are.

I devise two ways.

Look for screens in your life, these walls of protection you have built around yourself to keep you from tumbling in a downward spiral. How helpful are these? Can they be changed? We can devise ways to lessen their grip on our internal and external being.

Hold off doing this right at once, baby steps, remember. We start by easing up long-held-onto safety nets because we don't want the walls of our structure to come falling down.

Bringing wisdom into our lives can stop all the non-productive things that control our lives that really haven't got any true meaning. We begin to produce the things we need to get ahead.

Let's start this way.

What could be a good way to start the day? Exercise, a well-balanced breakfast, maybe not turning on the boob tube, as my mother used to call the television. Practicing meditation for a few short minutes in the morning. Go to that beach and feel all five senses, or if you like the mountains better then go to the top of a beautiful mountaintop and breathe in that oxygen of pure air, let it fill your lungs as you become one with nature. You are the master of your visual scene that takes you to your happy place, a place where you will learn to connect with what has been hidden in our esoteric world, a world without end.

THE MINDS OF
LEADERS PAST

I'VE SPOKEN TO SOME incredible souls in meditation and also in channeling.

When I began this chapter, I had in mind two things. To tell certain truths and to aid others in living their best life, so doing this, I got to speak to an incredible orator from another time in history.

Ben still has much to say and fills his time on the other side giving lectures.

He wanted to say to everyone reading this book, that it's okay to have doubts, and it's alright to have an open mind.

What I like to call an open-minded thinker.

He said research on this book cannot be aggressive because there isn't a lot that can be proven. God is not visible to us and neither is the other side, so concluding this, I will say, don't judge a book by its cover.

Divinity has a home and in this home is more than the human mind can imagine. Our forefathers knew this. They were more in touch with our reality than known in this country's history. The divine principles they were taught, led them to more honor than the later generations. The new generations have become more stagnant than previously before, you can blame this on technology, like many people say, and it is true.

If we could take time to look back in history, we could see

the honor our early politicians had. They had a great belief that this new country of theirs would show the world what a dignified republic could be. It started with the freedom to believe in a way of life that would be indulgent to all. Many critics of the Declaration of Independence believed that it could never stand up to the values they dictated. I believed in these words and held them deep in my soul and wanted this country to be great, free from the tyranny of an old and troubled crown.

We can all believe in God and Country, but do we give it the credit it deserves for we preserve the rights of all by taking those old words and making them new again? We can believe that the greatness of a country lies in its leaders, leaders for the sake of judgment who have become deceitful, and it is incredulous to the leaders of old to see the devaluation of a country that started with such greatness.

Emotion filled my eyes as Ben said these words, for I felt the emotions of disappointment and disillusionment Ben has for what has become. They fought with honor and valor for something that meant so much to the people of a country that was just beginning, and in leaving the company of this man, I was filled with awe and inspiration because even though this country has become a mess, I still believe in a time when men and women spoke with eloquence and grandeur in their levity.

After Ben's words, others came forward and wanted to share their thoughts. These incredible words came from Mr. Madison, a distant cousin.

The ancestors were taught a lot about honor and divinity and for their purchase, they were given the right to have free speech, and in their words; they had great honor. They sacrificed greatly for what they believed in and gave from the heart. If we can be taught to honor our mother and father, we can be taught to honor ourselves as well, and in doing this, we can contribute to society in a way that is giving and not just taking, for taking is allowing yourself to be above everyone else.

Yes, our ancestors struggled like all generations do, and in these struggles, they determined a way of life that meant they would work hard and give of themselves in a way a new country could flourish. They devised ways to fill their needs and be accessible to all.

We generalize too much of ourselves these days and the times of old have been forgotten. They seeded this land to fill the needs of not just themselves, but also for others.

The ancestors believe that today all has been forgotten, and what they started this country for, which is a country of jurisdiction and levity. The crime rates are out of control, the people of this country have become not only stagnant, but they have become coarse and raw, and in order for this country to become great again, it needs to start with a spark, an inspiration to everyone. Could it be in a new leader, someone who speaks from the heart and who is not so concerned about how much money they can make for their campaign, and who will not give in to the money grubbers and become people who lead with false promises? Gerrymandering at its worst.

You speak the words of the great minds because you avail yourself to their cause. We in the times of old could speak plainly and from the heart. We judged ourselves in a way that gave us theory and not bunk. We the people stood for something, there was idealism and the people listened to their leaders in awe. There was reverence and joy in these ideas that could take a country to heart, and if we continue to listen to false profits, then we will begin to become one of the low and externally undevout. In wording these judgments, I not only criticize the false leaders, but I also criticize the people who follow such shallow and immoral men and women.

We need to take heart in all of this nonsense, for in weakness, there can be strength.

When we look back at this time in history, those involved in propaganda will be reduced to the rumble they are.

The ones who speak of negativity are the ones to be wary of for in them is the disease of the mind that has led many a country down the road of imploding among themselves.

I would not want to upset anyone. This subject can be aggressive and maybe this all sounds critical; however, these words need to be shared, because, in them, you will see the truth and be beckoned to no longer be led by the throat.

Generating new beliefs toward a positive and higher functioning government could end so much of the strife that is spitting the country in half. If someone thinks their beliefs are right and you must bend to their ideals, fear this person for he is a fearmonger and only chooses to make you, his victim.

You are the creator of your own story and you must fight for the freedom to live the way you choose, and not be corralled into giving up your inalienable rights.

The time has come in America to speak up. Don't cower and say, I have no choice, for to do so is the beginning and the end of a country that began with a document that said free speech.

If someone tells you to destroy in order to get your wants and desires, fear this person, he or she is someone who is the mouthpiece of the devil. We can go on and on about what needs to change, but listen my dear fellow men and women, the change begins in you because you are not only an individual, you have a mind and a voice in the divinity of who your soul truly is.

My great-uncle Zach, had this to say.

I was a man once who had much to say, and in my words; I spoke my truths and said it best to my knowledge of a language of consent and determination to accomplish things no matter how hard, they took the world by storm and in the end as I grew weary, which came too soon, I saw that I'd committed not only acts that were wrong, but I saw my truths were strong.

In remembering my life, my niece has been tasked with the arduous task of speaking the language of old. She may not remember the times of the past, however, she seeks the governing voices of those who led before. I am reminded of the kindnesses that those in my life gave me, and I seek sort of a retribution in saying, I am sorry for the past. I seek not to change the ruefulness, however, to take them to task and remind the ones who now lead the charge to mind their p's and q's.

In my time, I could not see the forest through the trees. This was a time when all came to fruition by hard work and determination. If you see yourself in the position of President, then you need to take yourself to task and remember the people who got you in and not lead them astray, for if the multitudes of people put you in a powerful place, remind yourself they got me here, now give them thanks and praise.

One day I looked into the mirror and saw not the handsome young man I'd been, but a haggard man with a rough and not-ready look who must lead the country far, and instilled in me my father and mother gave of their hearts, and taught me the value of someone who takes the charge, even though I felt no longer robust and weary of war and travel. Now some may read between the lines and guess which leader I was. Just remember the language of old has no bounds, and if you speak with heart and truth, then you will go far.

Another distant cousin, Mr. Lincoln, said, we the people of the United States of America believed once in a country that was great. Modern organized religion has weakened this country, for in religion we should find strength and not failure in giving false nonsense, for in the falsification of these new profits of God come the devaluation of God's people. Presented with a false front of egotism and deceit, these low fear-mongering people have destroyed the very principles this country was designed for.

I hate to see divinity has become so low, for when I remember the sacrifices this country has given, it seems all was in vain. Fear not I say for in division there is strength in numbers. We must be allowed to think and speak from the heart again, for the leaders of this country have not heart. They have been lowered to the honor of skunks.

If you trivialize how you think, then you do not stand up for who you can become for the time is here that the people who should lead, are born with the intelligence and strength from within. I cannot repeat enough, the United States needs again to be united. This country has a world stage and the whole world is watching. If you hear discord and violence are prevalent in a country that is not so old, time and time again, you will start to believe in what you see and hear. You victimize the image that needs to be polished and fresh.

I would not conclude my words with anything less, your representatives represent you, the people of the United States of America.

Mr. Washington wanted to say, that we see ourselves the way we see others. If we see others as despicable then are we not despicable ourselves? We can win at this game called life. I once saw a great light in this country, and from heaven I see disparity and lies. The Greeks had it right. They could organize themselves in a way that could speak to the multitudes, to the people of their country that meant something to them because leaders were part of them and not above them. They did not give false promises, they gave hope.

I do not trivialize any of my words, I only want to see this country become what it once stood for, a people who could hold their chins up and see the value of being part of a democracy, instead of being part of a country of false prophets who gain for themselves, instead of giving to others.

The leaders of this country once stood up and gave notice to the multitudes of people who sacrificed everything they knew in their old countries and came here with hope and honor to give back to a country that allowed them to come in and work hard and pray the way they felt was right.

I once knew a time when the world was clean, it had just

begun. The air was fresher and the filth and betrayal of the war was over. The future was born with possibilities and the fields were filled with crops and hopes that all would be well.

We knew that in saying all people were created equal, lacked legitimacy for not everyone seemed to be included in that, and in the end, it led to another war, and worse yet, the decimation of the South had dire consequences which are still felt today by many. Now is not the time for discourse, however, it is a time of self-reflection and a time for all to come together, for in the now times there are others who seek to destroy, so in speaking this, I must say to the people of the United States to come together and respect each other and dig in and fight the new tyranny of distant lands.

Do not seek the pleasures of oneself, but seek the joy of giving to one another. The multitudes of people of different colors are just that, different colors. The color of a person's skin does not justify one's anger and resentment. We are one as a nation under God, and if I were among you today, I would seek to bring about change and not old tired resentments of a time long ago. Trust in yourself to be magnanimous in all you do.

Give hope, I say to the people of now for in them we see the future.

Mr. Jackson had much to say. If I were a man of honor and dignity, I would not give up the right to speak my piece, for in the words of a leader's past, there can be quiet dignity.

We, the leaders of the past, want to promote a future for our country as one of hope and continued freedom. I cannot give you an answer to what the future holds, only that with time and reason this country could prosper.

We hold these truths to be self-evident became a part of an important speech, a speech that is still read today. There was once a light in this country, a light that has dimmed with racism, greed, and overpopulation in underprivileged areas. Deceit runs rampant from the leaders.

I wouldn't categorize this country as rotten, only that it has allowed some of the principles it began with to lose their value. In promoting the future, the leaders need to have heart and dedication to the people who got them elected, for in them, you will see your future.

The strife has been building in recent years, and not all the early leaders of this country were perfect in any way shape, or form, however, certain people of the future present themselves with ego and self-serving principles that in no way would have been allowed in days of old.

If we generate enough steam that discredits others then others will join in the steady stream of lies and resentments that are instilled in that leader, who chooses to bring others into his discord and cheap attitudes.

A true man of leadership leads with integrity and not in frustration of an ego that is so big it rivals the size of the man's head.

When I led this country, I saw myself from the eyes of others. I knew they were watching, and I did not take the time to bring my own disillusionment to the forefront.

We can all look deep within and see that if our own thoughts are filled with the same rhetoric and incensement over things we cannot control; we all, however, can control our negativity and rile to a more positive and sincere conclusion.

We give in too easily to fearmongers and to people who have the most to say. We must take accountability for our actions, by getting to the truth.

MOBILITY OF THE MIND

M OBILITY OF OUR MIND starts with a conversation we have with ourselves, within ourselves. A start of a new idea, that spark of imagination that comes from deep inside.

Generations ago my own family contributed to society in many ways.

Recently, a spirit came to me and said his name was Makwa. In my mind's eye, I could see a Native American man with a strong jawline, and he said he was my Shawnee 7th Great-Grandfather. He was the father of Grandfather Tobi, whom I mentioned in the intro of this book. He told me he was a man who had a lot to say and no one listened to him. I had to laugh and tell him I could relate. I found myself connecting to this ancestor, who is telling me I have a deep lineage within the Shawnee nation. A vision of a woman popped into view and she told me her name was Wandering Tree and that she had been the Ojibwa wife of Makwa. Her father was the Ojibwa chief. For a brief few moments, I began to see the wonderful faces of my ancestors and of men on horseback.

He told me his father frowned on their love for each other and in the end, Makwa moved into the Ojibwa camp where he and Wandering Tree made their life together. He also furthered that there had been great strife between the European encroachers and the Shawnee Nation. The Shawnee grew incensed upon these new settlers taking their land, and making trouble for their people, and unfortunately, the rest is history.

I had no idea of my Shawnee DNA, only that a genetic test says I am one percent native.

Grandfather Makwa, said these beautiful words, "We all have principles, and depending on who you are in your life, you can rise to the occasion. If we allow ourselves to become bogged down and lose our curiosity, then we can go down the path of losing our way. If we are taught to listen to our heart and learn courage, then we can find our path to true happiness. In church on Sunday, we are taught the teachings of the Bible, however, we also need to be taught to listen to our hearts and minds. If we are taught to listen to our heart and learn courage, then we can find our path to true happiness. The soul knows who it is, and that knowledge comes from our ancestors, for they are as wise as the rivers run long and the stars go far.

If we galvanize ourselves into thinking about what has been lost to time, we can see from our own inner workings that we have just begun under the surface, a new embattlement within our own lineage, a lineage that goes back to the beginning of time. A spark that led to the current state we are in.

So, if we take this new knowledge, we might examine our own inner demons. These diseased thought processes that have kept us from doing what we must in filling the charts we wrote before the development of our embryo.

We had great designs on who this person would be before their life began. So, if we carry this chart with us, then why don't we try to tap into it and begin to understand why we came to the Earth school in the first place?

If we are at odds with ourselves and feel we cannot get ahead in this life, it could be we are out of touch with our charts.

The path of least resistance wins the ball. In this sports metaphor, I combine the litany of least resistance to be the winner of all. We need to get out of the primitive brain, sometimes referred to as our critter brain, that started in youth and did not always lead us down the right path. That part of the brain can reduce our chances of winning the game. It tells us to eat ice cream daily when we know we shouldn't. It tells us it is okay to play the losing game of self-doubt, it criticizes us into believing we are not worthy of love and understanding. If we fall into these long-held beliefs we learned in childhood, we forget the real you, the one who wrote your chart.

Examining our lives in the long run, we can now see how fallible it is to be human, the risk we take, the same risks our ancestors took long ago. Now knowing what our ancestors probably did not know, we can begin to change those old ways of thinking into new thinking, and new possibilities. It's a spark of the imagination to do this.

I hate to sound like I'm repeating myself, it's only to get the reader to develop a new understanding of the processes it takes to be human.

I have long held onto the idea of psychic ability, and this is why I probably developed my abilities; abilities my guides have told me I came into this life as a natural-born medium. This ability has been handed down for generations, and so, I have asked myself why my capabilities have become stronger than the previous generations. I think I have an answer to that. It's because I developed them, my constant fascination with what happens after death. Where do we come from and where do we go?

In our younger days, religion is the only thing that teaches us about such things. It's just, well, what religion teaches us is to be fearful of a God we cannot see, it teaches us going down the path of self-discovery and not serving the church's ideas on conventionalism, will send us down the path of self-destruction, and we could be shunned by the norm.

I find myself less concerned about being ridiculed by my peers as I go into the later part of my years, not that I'm announcing it to everyone who will listen. I have friends who I think the world

63

of and who would fall over if they knew the real me. This radical me. This truth-seeking and individual me who seeks comfort in knowing my ancestors, who are my friends on the other side.

Well, this may sound like I'm withholding my true self from these individuals I consider my friends. Not everyone is ready to hear this. This is simply not everyone's cup of tea, and that is fine. However, for the few that will read this book, I want to share the good news. We are not alone in the universe. We humans are from this fantastical dimension and from a fantastical immense population of light beings. Could it be, that we are extraterrestrial?

It sparks the imagination.

I advise all who read this, to examine your own life. What have been your contributions so far? What is your legacy? We come here of our own volition, no one forces us to come here. This is a free will contribution we give ourselves and to others for learning, learning to function in a world not of our own.

This world in which we come into can be rife with conflict. It can stagger the mind.

Such as the story of a fifteen-year-old boy who came to me this morning. In my dream, I was sitting next to an Asian boy and I told another person, I am sitting here with my friend, Tram. As I began to awaken, I saw awful visions of a boy curled up in a fetal position being beaten. He started telling his story. The Viet Cong had raided his village in Vietnam and began murdering everyone in it. After I helped release him into the light, he continued to tell his story. The carnage, he said, was so horrible that some of the forced soldiers did themselves in because they could not deal with what they had seen and done.

I told him how important it is to give his earthly trauma to God, which I tell all ghosts going home. Tram is now at peace in heaven.

Another morning, I had been dreaming a similar dream, where I sat across from an attractive man. Not the worst kind of dream, however, this man turned the other side of his face toward me and it looked mangled. I began to wake up and got his story. Probably sixty-some years ago, he was piloting a double-seated plane and it crashed. He had a young son at home and didn't want to leave him. I used psychology on him by saying the best way to see his son again was to go to the other side and wait to be reunited. He went.

We can be tangled in our traumas. They can whisk us away from who we are. Life can prove traumatic and if we put ourselves in others' shoes, we can see how good we have it, and yet, we squander our time here. I have allowed myself to think in the past that I am a product of what I've known, and where I've lived. These are the examples that have been given to me in my life. Did the adult figures in your early life teach you to be strong? Did they teach you what effort it would take to be the best you can be? If not, you can teach yourself what you need. You can parent yourself to success.

By understanding why we're here, and seeing our place in this world, we are reminded of what brought us here in the first place. To a place that can be wonderful, or a place filled with sufferings. We might think why in the world would we come to a planet rife with destruction? It can trigger an emotional response to think this way.

I find too little time is put into redefining who we've become, and it isn't too late to do so. Eliminate the things that are holding you back and you can find your way home.

Now, that we have concluded the idea of why we are here, let's take a look and prevent ourselves from fragmenting into a soul who is in their heavenly home, but for some unfortunate reason took that baggage with them that's holding them back.

THE FRAGMENTATION OF THE MIND

I N THE LAST CHAPTER, I spoke about the primitive brain, that part of the brain that holds us back from becoming that wonderful human being that started with an inkling of a life.

In each life we live, we can and probably will receive trauma. Trauma, if not dealt with, can destroy a beautiful mind, a mind that should by all accounts, conquer the world. If we live only for ourselves, and if we are demeaning to others, our souls can start to break, break into different pieces.

We may have fought in a war; we may have lost someone very close to us or had some emotional physical trauma done to us. These things can all lead to our soul fragmenting, a piece of us can break off and after our death can remain on earth, you've heard of a residual haunting. It can also have us not feeling quite like ourselves on the other side.

I recommend counseling before these things get out of hand. It takes great courage to face those inner demons.

I am a spirit counselor and spirit rescuer. I have dealt with all different types of spirits. I have helped with fractures. I have talked these poor fragmented human beings into the light. Many nasty ghosts come to me as they were in life.

The spirit of a woman heard me reading the part of this book about Christ to a family member who is helping with editing and began to scream at me about her fundamentalist beliefs. I've had the spirits of men, who have no respect for women, come into my house and say untoward things. Well, this book has many things, but I will not repeat the things I said to them.

How dare they come into my house and behave like they did on Earth. When you are a medium, souls come to you seeking help, they just don't always mind their manners, which can be aggravating, to say the least.

Luckily, I have the patience of Job and eventually help these lost souls.

So, if you have concluded the idea of what happens to us after death, you might want to deal with those issues holding you back, because if you don't, you may come into my kitchen someday and sing the song to me about what went wrong in your life, but hopefully not.

In my life, I've thought a lot about behavior. We all have difficulties. That's a fact of life. To err is human, to forgive is divine. In looking back on family dynamics, my own family was not spared these difficulties. Certain family members have been predisposed to anxiety and depression. I went through life thinking this was some genetically inferior grip on our family. How wrong was I? In talking with others, you can learn a great deal, like how these negative patterns run generationally. So, why do some family members have more issues than others? Why do they carry this sludge through their lives, while others live their lives so well? I can only say, from self-realization, the more focused *in* we are, the more miserable we'll be. Mind you, there is a little narcissism in all of us.

Remember others will let you down, however, don't let yourself down. Respect yourself. Everyone has ins and outs in relationships. People have pride and arrogance for a reason, it is to keep from becoming irrelevant. Stop being prideful. Pride is not a strong motivating force when it comes to relationships with others.

The less ego and pride you have the more people will like you.

There is more than one way to describe ego. Ego is an irrelevant term. Everyone has ego, it's just how you handle ego that determines if you are true to your divine self.

If you consider yourself better, smarter, and more attractive than others, and do it in a way you feel superior, then you have an inferiority complex. A truly divine person will see aspects of others that are not derivative of others. If you categorize yourself in a way that is equal and not superior, it is only because you see the best in others, and you are truly a person of open-minded perspective.

If others see themselves with dignity and respect toward their fellow man, then they can more easily align themselves with others. It isn't hard to see that in youth, we have to experience these things before we can truly see them and understand what they actually mean to us.

We contribute a great deal of satisfaction in our lives when we put others first, not meaning give your soul away, but remembering others came here for a similar purpose when they chose this life. If we tend to make enemies, it is because we don't give of ourselves and find the complexities in others as a trigger to make our ego apparent. Instead, realize we are not the only ones and others feel the same insecurities that we all do. It is indecent to think we are superior to others because we are in this world together, as a unit to unify this world into complacency.

Family dynamics does have a lot to do with ego. So many siblings don't get along. They fight for the hierarchy. The older wiser siblings, the middle-forgotten child, and last, but not least, the spoiled babies of the family, all wanting a piece of the puzzle.

So, in getting back to the sludge. How do we release it? I've learned to release it to the God energy. My way, of course, isn't the only way. I do believe with the help of a licensed therapist; we can get the help we need.

These fractures are from trauma. I've learned that genetically we are traumatized from the start. Genetic trauma from hundreds of years of family drama, past life trauma, and of course, the trauma of the life we are living now. In our now life, we might repeat the mistakes of the past, and it's important we don't because once we're back in our spiritual home, we might not want to sigh and say, "I better try it again."

It's best to face and accept these traumas. Forgiveness is huge, not easy. I'll discuss that later. These traumas can lead to fractures, and if we leave this earth, we could take that fractured part of us. Even though we are safely on the other side, these fractures can wear on us, until someone with abilities on the earth plane can break them and call them in, or sometimes, I understand with some hard work on the other side.

Like I said earlier, about a residual haunt, which happened with a little girl named Rebecca, who haunted my dolls' house. Our soul can make it to the other side and yet split. A soul can split or fracture and leave a lingering part of themselves.

My sister and I went to an old large house in Vincennes that is now used as a genealogy library. Hours were spent going through this wonderful collection of historical families' lives. I could feel the energy of an older lady who still thought of the place as her beautiful home. If walls could talk this house could tell the story of a poor young woman, who was married to an abusive man, who murdered her there.

Once at home, and around my dolls' house, I kept hearing an old French song and another childhood song. It was so strong only in that room with the house, and I began to feel the energy of a female childish ghost. In my mind's eye, I could see a little girl in a dress get too close to a fireplace. She later succumbed to her burns, and since her home was no longer there, Rebecca moved into the old house turned library along with several other neighborhood ghosts.

This tragedy from the 1870s had grounded her, and once I talked her over, I could still hear her songs, and a family member witnessed her shadow playing. My guide said she loved my dolls' house so much that part of her lingered there. It took some time and she is completely in her heavenly home now. She asked me to go back to the genealogy library to help her friends, and the beautiful French lady who'd taught her the song, to move on also.

There is a part of all of us that can linger on earth, and this will create a trauma to the soul, so in an effort to release this part of us, we must face our pain, the pain that led to the source of the trauma.

A relative read a newspaper account of a girl named Dona Maria Gonzales, who lived near early Vincennes centuries ago. The story went on to say this girl fell in love with a boy, who was not of the same status or the same culture. Her father decided to marry her off to a much older wealthy man, who was not so handsome. Dona Maria was mortified and destroyed by the idea and devised a way to get out of this marriage. She went to a local pond and walked into the still water and drowned herself. Locals have said for generations people can still hear her mournful cries.

Back to this relative. She called me quite excitedly, and remembered her life as Dona Maria. We went to the old pond, where we could see a beautiful quiet spot, that did not disclose the horrible sight of a woman in a white dress floating face down the villagers saw so long ago.

Just by going there, and facing that troubled life, healed her.

It does not take a lot to heal ourselves. We must face these traumas and accept them. God does help heal us and being sincere in our request can bring great relief. I would be remiss if I did not tell the secret to great happiness is to face our inner demons, those occurrences from so long ago in time that crippled us in a way that took our inner bliss.

In categorizing my own life, I can see my strengths and my weaknesses as an element to figuring out truths in my value system and my daily functioning self.

Withstanding, if we incur tragedy in our life, and that occurrence changes the trajectory of our life path, and if we allow these events to take shape in our life, we could stop functioning to the point of no return. We must say to ourselves, we need to let it go. Give it to the light of God. If we somehow contributed to the moment our life changed in this regard, then we need to say to ourselves, we are human, we are fallible, and if you need to say this to yourself several times through the day, then so be it.

If we allow life school tragedies to take hold of us, we cannot move ahead.

My own life has been fractured by things in my current life, but also from past lives.

A tragic event from my life as Catherine Martin, my 4th great-grandmother, came to light.

In the early 1800s, my 4th great-grandfather, William, came to visit the Martins with his father, Colonel Richard. When Catherine was around seventeen, she accepted the courtship of William. It was love at first sight for Cathy and Will.

Lucius Spragg showed up in the stable one morning where Catherine collected eggs, and being a hot-headed young man, he flew into a rage when she didn't accept his advances. Catherine's father, Captain John did not like his attitude and this brought out his ire, and unfortunately, Captain John thrust his fist into Lucius's stomach which caused a rupture. The blow ended the life of Lucius, and Catherine lived with the guilt of the incident.

Lucius visited me recently and said this incident fractured him, so I lit a candle and acknowledged the occurrence. Lucius told me this helped him and it helped me also.

With the help of William, I have brought memories of past lives into this life, and I would be remiss if I did not take care of them while I'm in the earth school.

There are many reasons why we carry such things.

In my training as a life coach, I've been taught the fundamentals of why we carry shame, shame that we have brought from childhood, things our parents did to shame us, or maybe teachers, or any other adult figures in our life. We can carry these into adulthood and they can rear their ugly head when we are trying to get our mental processes in order.

Do we crave certain foods, foods that are not good for us? Do we indulge and then feel shame, shame that we listened to our primitive brain, rather than listen to the logical brain that says just don't do it?

If we are an individual trying to break out of the shame game, then I will give you answers.

First, you must take control of that part of you that holds you hostage, and then you have to set up perimeters, or safeguards, to keep you from over-indulging, and not just food. These perimeters are called these anchors. What can these be? They can be a favorite song, or they can be a wonderful memory. Maybe positive notes around the house. My mother had a saying, nothing tastes as good as thin feels. Something that is going to get your attention and snap you back into reality, and steer you away from the primitive mind.

If you slip up and go back to that old way of feeling shame, then simply get back on the horse and begin again. Take accountability. It's not the end of the world, I can attest to this. I won't give up food I love, I just won't indulge every day. We must not deny ourselves, however, you've heard of too much of a good thing.

You will prove to yourself; that you can do whatever you put your mind to. This may sound like an old cliché, however, this is a simple and true statement, we are conditioned to flounder, and we are conditioned to win, to win in this game of life.

Believe in yourself. If there is not one person who believes in you, you have to find every reason in the world to believe in yourself. You are from an amazing place, and at this moment, you are not quite like your real self.

Picture yourself in a soft green meadow, and in this meadow, we lie down and look up at the sky and look at the rotating sun. The sun is bright and our eyes squint at the brightness. Tell yourself you are perfect, you were perfect at birth, not the imperfect person you were allowed to become. Now remind yourself of your divinity. Say to yourself, I am a true person of God, and I will not allow the imperfections of the earth school to continue to dictate who I am, this marvelous human being, who was brave enough to come to the earth and learn lessons I am taking home to lift myself to a higher vibrational being.

As you can see, I am broad-minded. Broad-minded to the point, I can see as far as the eye can see, well mentally anyway. I've sprung a lot of information on you to the point of no return, so I guess now I will teach you about feeling the need to seek approval from the other side.

APPROBATION OF
THE MIND

Logic. The 101 with logic is that you can never know the depths to which I seek, for in me are the constraints of long past. Of my past and your past.

We may seek answers, answers about our ancestors, now that we understand their importance in our lives. They really want to give you the knowledge they did not have, and in doing this, they can give guidance to the future generations, if there are to be any.

If we value the time we have left, we don't have to seek the approval of the ancestors, however, we do need the approval of ourselves. Could we be letting ourselves down, that soul self who wrote the contract? In answer to that, yes. Yes, we do need the approval of ourselves more than we need the approval of others.

As I tell spirits I move on, don't worry so much about what the ancestors think about you on the other side, because you are being harder, than you know, on yourself. This is why many souls get stuck. Makes sense doesn't it, that they are worried about that Christian God who seeks to hold you accountable for all the despicable things you did on earth. They ask themselves; will I be sent into some hellfire and dig coal for the rest of eternity? And I can tell them, no, you will not bear the chains of the selfish life you lived for eternity.

You may though, as I said, carry that fracture.

A clue to what happens to the soul who does not deal with

these self-inflicted or happenstance traumas. You will return to the heavenly realm and encounter issues that came with you from that life, or any other lives you lived.

I know this from speaking to my ancestors.

An ancestor, a third great-grandfather, Zach. I remembered the love I had for him in my life as his mother. Harsh things happened in his life one hundred and seventy years ago, and when speaking to him, he held back. For some reason, I wanted to seek his approval, and I thought he was angry with me for leaving him in that life, which is another story, I began to think. I know the things that happened to him from family research, things I wouldn't wish on anyone, especially him.

Could it be? Could it be, that these traumas weren't dealt with correctly, leading to his soul to suffer on the other side? I've since learned he's lived other lives after the traumatic life.

My family and I tried to find the grave site of this plague-ridden community and could not, so instead, we went to his son's gravesite and used the medicine bowl and prayers to call in his soul to be whole again. I can sense he feels at peace now.

After this, my ancestors began to teach me about fractures, and I have learned much since. We all can carry them, so the next question is, how do I prevent them?

THE DENSE MIND

THE ILLOGICAL MIND THAT is too dense to allow anything in, except working, what I'm eating, and what I'm watching on television this evening. Not that television is a bad thing, it can be a teaching tool, however, when we fill our minds with negative images, negative images from the six o'clock news, images of murder, and violence, this can take away from the self we were really meant to be.

Why do young men seem so violent? When you fill your time playing violent video games, and watching violent movies, perhaps, you lose the logic of the real world, yes, a world that can be violent sometimes, however, you contaminate that frontal cortex that could lead you to success. So, I would say to parents everywhere, get your young children into activities, activities they would enjoy. If they enjoy art, get them art lessons, if they like sports, by all means, get them into sports. Just something that is going to spark that genius, that frontal lobe.

In other words, watch what you put into your mind, for that could lead you down the road to that fracture we've been talking about.

I find, that we as humans, tend to marginalize our lives to the point of no return. I encourage you, as the reader, to allow that spark of genius to the forefront. Allow it to take precedence over the piddly things in our life, the things, if we take a closer look, don't seem quite as important as they once did.

Varied knowledge comes from two different principles. The first, available knowledge is the information we have at hand, and idealistic knowledge refers to the knowledge we do not have at hand. Idealism, the true form of self-defeat. I encourage you to read this line carefully. If we stick to an idea that we feel can't be changed, it becomes static, and sometimes this can be dangerous if we become resistant to change our belief. We must ask ourselves, where did this belief come from? Is it logical? Are my views on this belief supported? Is this something I know to be true? And if this belief becomes too radical, and you find yourself unable to give an inch, and if you find like-minded individuals, you might see a form of radicalism. A view that can have religious constraints or psychological restraints.

Any way you look at it, many radicalized individuals can become dangerous. We see this more in other parts of the world, however, take a look at the country you live in. Do you see groups of people who have unrealistic principles that feel they are superior, and for some reason, feel the right to tell you how to live your life?

In this new age, this way of thinking undermines the logical thinker. The person who is open-minded, but does not feel the need to tell everyone else how to live. We have become a culture of people programmed to believe the person who gets on the highest pedestal and professes they have the answer. These dangerous individuals can rise to supremacy because they have some hypnotic power over people who are not open-minded. One man I speak of was Hitler. So, if you find yourself glorified over these not-well-formed individuals, back away.

There is a dogma about the lust of an individual who speaks negatively to the masses.

And now I rest my case.

If we stimulate the dense mind, we can start to spark that wonderful imagination. I find the theory of relativity can cover so many issues. This idea that things are not static, and if we prescribe ourselves to the mobile mind, the thinking mind, we can do much, so much more in our lives than we ever dreamed possible.

THE DREAMER'S MIND

W E SOMETIMES FIND OURSELVES disgusted with the daily grind. Every minute of the day filled with menial tasks. Once upon a time, before a profession, before marriage, before children, we might have had that creative imagination that took our thoughts by storm. This excitement that took hold of unlimited creative thinking. Just think if you could have made those dreams a reality. I'm not saying to quit your job or drop your marriage and children, I'm only saying that if you still have an inkling of that creative dream, why not slowly begin to put it into action? Maybe take a few minutes of each day for yourself and work on that which can make you happy.

Some of us might find ourselves consumed by it, and see our real life take the backseat, so of course, we have to keep hold of our logical mind and say to ourselves, I must do this in small steps. Anything big and overwhelming is much easier to do in small steps.

Creative genius did not probably consume our ancestors. They probably stuck to the daily grind that filled their long days. Not giving in to that dream. Thinking it was more important to their families to bring home the bacon and fry it up in a pan.

Well now, if this makes us think. What if I do quit watching a not-so-favorite television program that helps me unwind at the end of the day, and take that time for productivity toward that dream?

I can attest that I have done this.

We are creatures of habit; we like our safe routines because getting off our daily patterns can leave us flustered. So, why not look at getting away from routine? The secret of getting out of your rut and seeking new adventures is to take your desires and make them part of your normal routine.

Change your way of thinking and let your imagination run free.

This paragraph is a keeper.

It really comes down to learning how to change the primitive brain. This is the hardest thing we humans can do. What about that diet and that desire to fit into a size eight again, and what about the exercise habit you've been saying for eons you planned to do? We all have patterns in our lives, and most of these habits were started in our youth.

Back to the ancestors. I know many of my ancestors were farmers. They worked hard in the fields from dusk until dawn with little complaint. It's just how it was back then. At night they would collapse in their bed, rise at the crack of dawn, and get up and go again. They had big families, so, well, maybe they didn't go straight to sleep, anyway, this led to a lot of mouths to feed, and this is not much more than a hundred years ago.

So, what happened? Most of us aren't farmers anymore. We have nine-to-five jobs, and smaller families, and still we struggle, struggle to find that balance. What is eating up our time?

It goes back to the old saying, 'If life were easy, we would have no challenge, and without challenge, we would have no lessons, and without lessons, we would have no purpose.'

Could it be, that we aren't challenging ourselves? We are so much into our stability that we forget our purpose here on earth is to learn, to learn as much about ourselves and the world around us. This big beautiful orb in the sky spinning around the sun.

Did we always want to learn Spanish? Do we secretly desire to get into the new Pickleball craze? Well, these are only a few things, we could be doing, so why not take time once a week? Small steps.

I'd advise not to wait. I have long held onto the belief our time is limited on our plane of existence, that our time here on earth is brief, even if we live for a hundred years.

By the way, my guide revealed it feels like weeks til they see us again.

To find the truth about what we have designed our lives to hold most important, then we must think back. Think back to a time when the hands went slowly around twelve numbers.

As kids, time went by slowly. I always heard people say, just wait until you get older, time goes so much faster. Wow, I typed that and the second hand made two revolutions. Oh, maybe that's because I'm not the best typist.

Anyway, if you find yourself lacking time, it could be you are not making the most of your time. If we look at everything we do in a day, could it be some things aren't so important? What if we didn't wash those two dishes in the sink, and instead, put those couple of minutes into something more productive, like finishing that painting, or finishing that novel, or maybe taking that walk and getting some exercise? Our brains are trained to do menial tasks, and could it be these tasks are getting us off track to accomplish the things that will make our lives more complete?

I wonder. Are these little things keeping us from some of the big things?

So, again I will stop my rant and move on to the next.

THE OBSERVANT MIND

SOMETIMES IF WE FEEL the walls are closing in on us, we can observe that our mind is perceiving something is amiss. Is this a sign something is going on in our mental processes? Are we overwhelmed, underwhelmed, or maybe even both?

If we limit our time to our everyday things, we may feel unease. Could we just need a vacation from the grind? If this is so, we might be someone who needs to take a breather, a break from demands. And if I asked you why you felt this way, you may reply, I'm just not getting everything I need in life.

That is a legitimate reason. I encourage you to take that vacation. In all fairness, our boss should be open to workers taking a break, because if they don't take a break, they might break, and that would not be good for anyone.

I appreciate there are times in a company, that it isn't a good time.

I have good friends and family who are or have been nurses, and the wonderful people in that profession have taken up the slack for the ones who left the profession. And why you ask? Because they are in one of the most demanding and under-appreciated fields. Why would you stick around and be treated like a second-class citizen, and be told if you take more than three days off in a year, you won't receive a raise? That happened to my cousin.

Well, that's enough of that, almost. Nurses are saints.

They all deserve a raise.

Sometimes in our lives, we feel like we are up a tree. What I mean by this is literally like feeling you are up a creek without a paddle. These are metaphors of course, however, when your life has become so complicated, you don't know which end is up, or which end is down, and then we need to look back and say, where did things go wrong?

When I was young, I believe I lived a life of seeing the cup half full. Again, with the metaphors. It's only that as children, we are of a purer mind. We haven't lived through terrible things, hopefully, and if we have, kids do seem to have a way of rebounding faster. Judging from a good upbringing, you will more likely rise up more quickly.

Now we've talked about this before, the idea that our lives are not static. They indeed have a vibration to them. Conquering self-doubt, and encouraging one-self to identify why we choose to live in circumstances that are not productive to our way of living. I understand there are things beyond our control that can send our lives spiraling off course.

With this, guidance can come from the other side, and we just need to know how to access this help from our loved ones in the next plane of existence. They are there, free for the taking is the advice they would love to give us. Not all advice is for everyone, they can be fallible, however, their advice can be spot on. I trust them. Have not always agreed, but choose to agree to disagree.

When we think about our ancestors, they begin to follow our lives, probably some more than others already have been following what we do. At first, this can feel a little fear-inducing because we don't like to feel we are being watched. Relax, they are not watching our every movement, and plus, they have lived lives, and they are actually pretty open-minded.

In spending time speaking with the ancestors, I find I enjoy their company, they give me a run for my money with their jokes, for they are quite funny. We all feel them around us from time to time, and it is very much a comfort to know they're with us.

Developing habits that can bring about true communication is truly not that difficult. You will find that just talking out loud is a way of starting a conversation. You may not hear them at first, still this begins a dialogue, an opening in an old and wonderful relationship.

Our ancient ancestors had observant minds. We can tell by the things they left behind.

Ancient monoliths, the pyramids around the world, the native American petroglyphs carved into mesas and caves, the henges in Europe, including the most known, which is Stone Henge. Many of these ruins are designed to be in position of a certain planetary and star alignment. So many ancient ruins tell a tale of people, early modern man, that they were quite adept in the knowledge of astronomy. Where did they get this knowledge? Could it simply be that they had a lot of time on their hands to put all their energy into watching the skies? After all, they didn't have electronic devices that they stared at from dawn until dusk.

There are so many mysteries about our origins, and where we come from.

Many a man has questioned this. Did they have help? A rag-tag group of people have become known as the ancient alien theorists. Swiss author, Eric Von Daniken wrote about this in 1968 in a book called, Chariots of the Gods. People familiar with this book know that many question if these pyramids and other ruins were built by aliens from other planets, after all, how did men stack huge boulders into place? Whether these theories are founded, I do know if you are observant, you begin to see things that others can't. It makes you think.

I've seen unexplained unidentified aerial phenomena in the sky, and I know others who have. My own parents witnessed a round disc-shaped glowing object sitting in a field as they drove across an overpass in Illinois. This was 1958, a time when we were only beginning to talk about such things. They said it looked exactly like the reported version of an alien craft.

I find that the observant thinker has the ability to see farther, farther into things others are simply too busy to take the time to see.

If we all took a little time to be more plugged in, more observant, then you too could begin to see that life is more than meets the eye.

Over the years, I've met a lot of ghosts, however, very few times have I observed an actual visual ghost. Twice in my young life did I realize something was different. This happened when I turned eight years old. My mother named our Siamese cat, Pyewacket, which means witch in Old English, and after the Siamese cat from the movie Bell, Book, and Candle, a 1958 fantasy romantic comedy movie starring Kim Novak and James Stewart. Anyway, my tomcat got out of the house and never returned. Someone had seen him on the highway. A few days later, I was playing outside and looked up at the side of our little house and saw his face floating mid-air. Even though I loved my cat, it terrified me because you are not supposed to see these things.

I found out a short time later that you not only can observe with sight, but you can also observe with your ears.

Our house became too small for five people, so in 1972, my parents purchased a large two-story home, which was one of the oldest houses in our little southern Indiana town. I remember my mother asking the current owner if the house was haunted.

She replied, "Only by us."

On our moving-in day, I came inside the house and looked up at the twelve-foot ceilinged staircase, and put my foot on the step to look for my little brother. At the top of the stairs, I went toward his bedroom and heard heavy footsteps following me up, and when I turned to look, I saw no one there, and the only way to get away was to run back downstairs.

I found out I had been the only person in the house.

The observer questions, did I imagine that, or was there a scientific answer for it.

Well, I cannot be sure, however, the house turned out to be haunted.

An old fort just north of Vincennes, Indiana, has some family history to it. Our third great-granduncle Zachary led the fort in the early 1800's. We discovered a horrible story that happened there. My sister, also an observer, and uses more than her normal five senses, wanted to hike one day, and asked if I'd go along. She mentioned the presence of a menacing Native American man who showed himself as a wolf another time she hiked there alone, or could it have been the dreaded Skinwalker?

Well, no wonder she wanted me to go with her.

"Why not move him to the other side," I said. I tend to go places others stay away from. I enjoy going to places where others won't and am one to not back down.

She took me to a dried old gully where anyone with any sensing abilities could feel him. We stood there, and I spoke. I told him he had kept great care of the land long enough, and he should go where he would find love and redemption for anything he'd done. He would also see his family and friends again. My sister repeated he needed to be with his family. After some contemplation, he made his decision. I'm not sure what happened, I only knew this great emotion that came from him. I said, "The tribe is here." They came for him. It felt so overwhelming, I've not felt such emotion when aiding a spirit into the light. I cannot imagine being away from family and friends and seeing them again after so long.

What a powerful moment.

The next day in my kitchen, I felt a strong spirit come around me. I asked if it was him. He said yes, and when I asked him his name, he told me Thundercloud. Over the next few days, he revealed more of his story. He was the son of a Piankashaw chief. I knew about the Piankashaw Natives from the neighborhood of our old house in Vincennes, supposedly built on the land of the Piankashaw, and my grandmother had lived in the Piankashaw apartment building. They were a great tribe in that area for millennia.

His story so tragic.

He, his cousin, and some other braves went out as a hunting party along the Wabash River. Earlier, a group of Delaware were coming down the Wabash and spied two of the fort's soldiers, also hunting. They captured them and tortured them by making them run the gauntlet. In my mind's eye, I was shown a handsome Spanish American man, named Franco. I could see him saying they took away my dignity.

Anyway, the Piankashaw hunting party was set upon by some of the forts' soldiers, and mistaken for the natives who had brutalized their compadres. The soldiers enraged by the mutilated bodies of their friends, came across the Piankashaws cooling off in what is now the dried old gully, and the soldiers took their rage out on the peaceful hunting party.

One tragedy gave way to an even greater tragedy. The story is lost to time. I find no proof of this story's existence, only the feelings and knowledge I was given.

The spirits like us to tell their stories, I have learned.

Over the days of hearing his tragic tale, Thundercloud's energy became frantic.

He told me about his cousin, Running Wolf. He did not take my encouragement to go the other side, because he did not trust this white woman, who came into the forest claiming there was a better existence, and so he remained and fell into a bad state of mind from losing his cousin. I felt like jumping in my car, and going back, but couldn't just leave and drive the distance, especially with work.

Later, on a Friday morning, along with my sister, and a friend, we returned to the old fort.

Almost immediately, I could feel his energy, and heard him yell, "The *enemy.*" It was me who'd taken away his cousin. That week Thundercloud repeated a phrase he wanted me to tell

Running Wolf. He felt if he heard this native tongue word, he would understand it came from his beloved cousin, Thundercloud. *Meo ho* was the phrase. He said it meant the language of love.

Once I said the phrase, used the medicine bowl, and together we said some Christian prayers, the spirits went over. My guides told me not just Running Wolf went, but also the two soldiers, Franco, and the other man whom I never learned his name, a soldier who had been murdered by another soldier, a fever victim who died in the fort, and another couple of native Americans.

After I left this area, a poem came to me. 'The sun and moon cross the sky, now dawn lingers in the distance. The fingertips of the moon waiver, as the din of morning dulls the sky.'

And now we go from the observant mind to the fierce mind.

THE FIERCE MIND

W E CAN TRULY BE guided by these ancestors of ours. They are more than our counterparts; they are a true host of friends. I like to compare them to our friendly hosts in the sky.

Not that they come from the sky.

Our fierce mind can be protective, it can protect us from ourselves, and others. It is that part of the mind that senses when there is danger. That feeling, and sense, that warns us when there is a possible case of doom headed our way.

Well, that may sound dramatic, however, have you ever wondered if that voice is our favorite grandfather, warning us of life's dangers? What if that extra sense, we feel, is guided by the ancestors? Wouldn't those family members, who have since moved on, want to protect us?

We've all had a moment in our life where we've had that extra-sensory perception, and in that moment, have you wondered, could it be? Is it a gut feeling, or something more profound?

I can attest to the fact, that yes, our ancestors strive to protect. Of course, not everyone has the ability to hear. I'm clairaudient, which is the auditory version of extrasensory perception. I am also empathic, which is a heightened feeling of sensing.

So, if these ancestors fiercely want to protect us, wouldn't they want to guide us to make good choices? My son hears his spirit guide, who is his third-great grandfather, Henry Beck. My son gets so annoyed when Grandpa Henry urges him to make better choices.

We all have a fierce mind. Only some of us have it more profoundly than others do.

I have witnessed this many times in my life, this fierceness that can penetrate the soul. We are divine in ourselves, and we want to prosper; however, many do not know how to go about it.

If we learn to use our fierce mind, that protective part, we can lose out on many things that will make our lives so much better. Our protective mechanism can outweigh the senses we need to get ahead, for aren't we at our best, when we give worry to the wind?

I contribute this part of the mind to a long-learned process that we've gained in primitive times. Not so much as defending oneself from a sabertoothed tiger, which could have occurred.

I am talking about the part of our brain that kept us alive and well and gave us knowledge that fire is not safe. We respond to things, we have concluded, that are not good for us by staying away from them.

Now our logical brain tells us fire, if handled correctly, can give us warmth, and fire can cook our food, so it does not kill us, and so, the logical brain can be balanced with the fierce brain, and this tells us how to prevent danger, and still get on with our life. We need this balance to give us credence to our inner ambitions. We can stay safe, and yet with logic, we can circumvent our worries and work our way to success.

Worries and fears can prevent us from good choices, these choices we make to pay the bills, put food on the table, and raise our families in a happy environment. Fear resonates with all of us. We fear life sometimes more than we live it.

The fierce mind seeks to protect. It protects us from ourselves in not all bad ways, however, in ways we deceive ourselves. If we take control of the fierce mind and do not allow it to work in a way that keeps us from dividing and conquering our own hopes and dreams, then we can be pragmatic, and seek new answers, answers that have been limited to us by our protective brain.

I would always give everyone the benefit of the doubt and encouragement to focus on self-esteem issues, whatever issues are holding you from accomplishment.

I ask you to reason with that fierce mind, tell it its contributions have been useful, and now, I direct you to say to the fierce mind, we are now going to set it aside enough to give us some breathing room, some room to focus on other needs. I am not going to play with fire, I am only going to light my imagination with creativity and the things I have desired to do for so long.

A MEETING OF THE MINDS

O NLY RECENTLY DID I discover my soul mate.
In my search for William, Catherine is a life I did not remember until much later in my life. My soul mate helped me remember.

During the Covid years, I had more time on my hands and decided to use this time to do family research. One side of my father's lineage fascinated me. For years the family said a famous United States President was part of our lineage. Could it be?

During my research, I discovered the president's brother, William, was my direct 4th great-grandfather. I needed to find birth certificates, or marriage certificates in order to put these records into the historical societies for these old well-known families. Kentucky did not keep records until much later, so I spent hours poring through old records on the internet. So much so his name appeared on my most searched bar at the top of the computer.

One morning I woke to see a man standing at the end of my bed, and for some reason, even though I had no idea what he looked like in life, I knew who he was, my grandfather, William. It was brief, I had the strangest attraction to him. Yes, attracted to my grandfather, how strange, I had to laugh, or was it cringe?

From that time, we began to communicate. He took over as my main spirit guide, although Mon Ami had been my female guide for years, and then began my ability to communicate with other ancestors. As shocking as these communications were, they became amazing. I learned much about my heritage. And yes, they told me, your father's grandmother was from that amazing family. Grandma Martha's grandfather, William, and Catherine's son, Zachariah, died in a plague with his wife, Nancy, and so their four sons, spared in the plague, went to live with their maternal grandmother, and in a way, lost connection with this incredible lineage, which goes back to the Lee's of Virginia, the Mayflower, and to royal ties in England and France.

And so, I learned to speak to the ancestors, which is pretty mind-boggling in itself.

Back to searching for records on William, I asked to speak to his wife, Catherine. He became quiet and finally said I couldn't because she was in another life. What happened next was one of the most amazing things to happen in my life. I said out loud, and to myself, because thankfully no one could hear me, "Oh my God, I am Catherine, and you and I are soul mates."

Lily was difficult to remember, Catherine left me mumbling incoherently for several weeks.

It couldn't be, my grandfather, William, and I were soul mates, and we had been settlers for ten amazing years in a life together in the early 1800s in Louisville, Kentucky. Like Lily, Catherine died in her middle twenties. William told me Catherine had an ectopic pregnancy, and even though he was a surgeon, he could not save her. Unfortunately, surgery and medicine weren't that far advanced. It was a tragedy for him and our son.

William has shown me parts of their life together. If it wasn't for him, I probably wouldn't have known. Seeing these images seems familiar, and there is no way I could feel these intense emotions unless I lived them. I don't cry easily, but when I remembered her death, I cried like a baby. After all, I had been with my soul mate and had a young son I adored. Our son is my 3rd great-grandfather.

Yes, we often reincarnate in our same family lineages, although not always.

I've learned other family members are a reincarnation from our past grandparents who lived several generations back. It seems every three or four generations or so, although my oldest son is his dad's older brother. My sister is Forest Woman, our Ojibwa and French 4th great-grandmother, and my son is our French grandfather, Jean Dejarnet, who came to this country around 1700, and Jean's second great-grandson, Christopher.

I am grateful every day for William. He teaches me so much and I can hear him better than I can hear my other ancestors, *usually*.

Staying close to what we know on the other side can help us. Each generation brings something to the plate, so to speak. These ancestors may have trivialized their lives on earth, but trust me when I say. We are no trivial beings.

Each one of us represents a part of the puzzle. A piece of the pie, so to speak, of an incredible race. We may find our lives dull or void of excitement, however, the other side is anything but dull. We may watch television or go to movies to fill that void. This gives us a chance to live vicariously through other people, however, if you believe in the processes I've been speaking of, isn't that what we are doing, playing a role in our lives, so why not make this your own movie, why not live life to the fullest while we are here.

Not everybody has it in them to live a dynamic life, or has money, so why not make it the best way for yourself? You can contribute to life by just being present. Giving to those who cannot take care of themselves, by contributing to mankind, you are extending the greatest part of yourself.

If I could give an example of altruism, I would give you someone who is truly deserving of sainthood. These people are the soul and spine of who we should be. To be altruistic means we are giving, giving back to others. Altruism doesn't just mean giving back, it means we are the divine students of the other side.

I fear others are feeling a lack of altruism these days. In the earth school, we have become so riddled sometimes by negativity, that we often forget our true divine selves. We go on in life fearing it because we were never allowed to just be ourselves, and when this happens it can lead us down the road of being self-defeating. I don't mean to sound negative, it's just that we are so wrapped up in our grief of things that happened in the early stages that we cannot even conceive of our own reality.

We may find the very thought of getting out there terrifying at first. In doing so, you will begin to see yourself in a new role. It isn't rocket science to extend yourself to others, but in the long run, you will see a you that fits the bill.

I encourage others to get out there because if you don't, you may not fill the chart you so eagerly wrote before you came to earth. I'm told I've already filled mine. This is one of the reasons I wrote this book, and why I felt the need to give back what I've been taught.

Getting back to the meeting of the minds, if we find ourselves divided on time, we can simply place the blame on the manifold of things in our lives that keep us off track of this daily game of life. If you are one of the few who have conquered keeping the daily grind straight, then you are a person with a high degree of success, because we cannot be successful if we don't meet this issue head-on. We rely on ourselves to get everything done, however, what if you shared the day-to-day things you need to get done? Why not share in responsibilities? Most of our families probably have two arms and two legs. You'd be amazed at what you can accomplish with one limb. Ask someone who does.

We stake the responsibilities on the female member of the family to get everything done, so in the name of keeping the sanity of this particular family member, please help in doing some dishes.

Regarding this, I can see that my efforts are great. We take great effort in trying to bring our achievements to where they should be, the finished projects of a mind that can take responsibility in their daily grind.

We should worship the people in our lives who can ascend to great lengths to get the things done in order to move on to other things.

It is a no-brainer to get things done, however, if we suffer from anxiety and depression, these trivial responsibilities can seem like an uphill battle. We feel we are moving through sludge. Things that one day feel like a breeze, and other days seem like a momentous task that requires the efforts of a herd of elephants.

If you are one of these people, please see someone who can get us past these obstacles, and help lead us down the path of a more rewarding life.

The proper psychologist can figure out why these traumas have depleted your life existence. It is also possible for someone trained in the holistic trade to bring an individual to self-improvement and can get you unstuck from what is holding you back.

If I were someone battling these issues, I might try first a holistic practitioner who deals with such problems. Some are trained in the art of reducing some of the trauma and neglect you received in your youth.

Being a whole-minded person in the earth school is important because, without help, we cannot finish what we came here to do.

THE OBLIGATE MIND

THE PERSON WHO HAS an obligate mind is an adversary to some. We look at this person with a degree of civility, however, if this person is transparent enough for us to take a good look at, we will see a less-than-productive person. The reason this person affects us differently than others is because they give us no clue to the truth that is within them.

I would never ignite this person into a battle with words only because they would go into verbal weaponry that would leave you flat. They will coerce and require you to side with them, and they can be cunning, to say the least.

I'd advise anyone who is of the obligate mind to take a deep look at themselves because if they don't, they might find themselves with a soul fracture. Trust me when I say, I have helped people with this mindset to the other side.

When they find that others don't agree with them, they will immediately find fault. For the sake of friendship, maybe don't always feel the need to be right.

The reason I felt the need to write about the obligate-minded person is to lessen their chances of gaining a soul fracture, and if I could get one person of this mindset to see themselves, then I have helped.

Our ancestors were quick to find fault with others, simply because they were human. We all find fault with others, but usually not to the degree of some. Choosing a path of least resistance can also lead you to a path of harmony.

In writing this book, I try to engage the mind to see the different types of people there are and have always been. The earth school is a place of great learning and of great women and men who have preceded us. We see their contributions they have given to their descendants.

Again, I say, we carry the torch, so where can this take us now? It can take us to a corner of existence we never knew about, the existence that contributes to a lot of our learning, whether we realize it or not.

We can get a lot of flak by simply being who we want to be, a productive citizen on the world stage. To others, it might seem obtrusive and uncomfortable for them to understand, and to the mindset of the less creative, you will see this as bunk.

This has simply to do with the flag they carry.

THE INDISPENSABLE MIND

I N OUR LIFETIMES, WE regard ourselves as humans. A rare breed of logical thinkers, designed to learn and to work and play, if they are the indispensable thinker.

I would never raise anyone's hackles, to disregard the multitude of people generally staying in an immobile state of existence. If you are one of these people, I advise you to get up and keep moving because things in motion tend to keep moving, and it is crucial to our mental and physical health to keep busy. We, as human beings, are meant to be active.

With this in mind, I suggest to the reader of this book to keep going because you are not dead yet. Now, that may sound harsh, but it is in no way meant to be mean.

What I'm saying, is we should keep active in our lives and then we can achieve some of those things we intended to do from the start. It's the key, the essential part of us that can give us these things we desire in this lifetime. Not necessarily the lottery numbers, however, the required tasks we need to fill the charts we created. Yes, it is you who creates your chart. No God or deity is forcing you into these lives as a penalty for your penance.

We are here of our own vocation, no one puts a gun to our head. We want these lives, and we desire to learn and repeat different lives so we can learn different things each time. In my work, early on, I had no idea what the future held for me. The more I began to work with my guides and especially my guide,

William, the more I found myself beginning to see more meaning in my life, and the more I began to help lost spirits, even better things appeared in my life.

I cannot say I ever doubted the other side existed, I just didn't realize the ancestors were more than ready to answer my questions with their knowledge and help in understanding my life and purpose. For me, anyway, once the ancestors became part of my daily life, I began to see myself more clearly, through their eyes. They didn't judge me. They only want to protect and guide.

Now training yourself to connect with the part of you that wrote that chart is not as hard as it sounds. The conclusions you will learn at the end of your life will show you how you could have done things differently. You may see that you lived a selfish life and gave to yourself more than others. So, how can you change the irresponsible things you do in your life before it's too late? I will tell you.

Take a good look in the mirror. Do you like the person you see? Is this person giving or is this person taking? What are the contributions you are giving in this life?

If you say, I am there for others and I make it my supreme responsibility that the people around me are thriving and living a life by what they have been taught by example, then I would say, you are winning this game.

If you say, I am controlling, and I try to victimize the people around me, then stop. If you are so afraid of losing everyone around you, that the people in your life get sucked into this abuse they can't get out of because they are afraid, then seek help, and learn how to handle your anger management.

Many individuals from certain groups of beings have considered our progress to have been beneficial to some and not to others. This has to do with value systems.

If what we live for on earth is for ourselves, then we can't begin to own the choices we made in the progression of our lives. Progress comes in different forms. When we undergo changes to our life path arbitrarily, we will see our defense mechanisms have kept us from getting ahead in life.

I guarantee if we make better choices, we will contribute in some way to our fellow man, and this is where we can divide and conquer fears, and idleness, to keep ourselves from becoming too complacent.

I suggest many ways to do this. First, we have to come to terms with what is holding us back. This can be a variety of things, such as disorderliness, or maybe some of the other deadly sins. Clutter can be a big contributor to our self-management because if our surroundings are in chaos then our minds are also in the grips of disorder. If we can get rid of the things that are holding us back, we will begin to see things in a new light. By lightening the load, we as humans actually thrive in our lives. Less is best.

This can be done in small steps. Make piles of things to keep, things to send to one of many of the organizations designed to take our unwanted items for resale, and things we'd like to sell, and last but not least throw trash in the trash.

The key to getting our lives in order is to get our brains in order. We change our way of thinking and we will begin to see positive changes. We have to *want* these things that will change our lives for the better, and I encourage you to make daily notes and be committed to your path to success.

Again, I sound like I'm repeating myself, however, the more we are reminded, the bigger chance we will have to become the person we want.

Now, you may wonder what this has to do with the ancestors, and I will tell you. Our ancestors were designed to get ahead. They didn't have the technology we have today. They didn't have interference with telephones and modern devices. Life was simple. They knew they had to work in order to live. To have a roof over their head and enough food, they had to make haste, not waste.

Today in society depression seems to run rampant among our youth. They have little direction. Our ancestors, even children worked on the farm, there wasn't time to be depressed, they were too busy. The constant looking at our devices can depress a happy individual. As an example, if we read daily how wonderful everyone's vacations are and we go nowhere, then we are bound to be depressed.

When we are young, we also see ourselves as indestructible, of course, this is not logical because as we know human beings are fallible, we can break, physically and mentally. If we are not given what we need in order to grow as a person, then we could go down that rabbit hole of self-destruction, and this may not be immediate in our early life, however, gradually this can lead us down the path of our self-alienization.

I'm not suggesting we give up our cell phones, our computers, and televisions, maybe limit ourselves to the time we put into them. Now, I cannot imagine, we are programmed to want to live vicariously through others, however, society today, in a way, teaches us to not be ourselves, it teaches us to be less than what we are, these divine human beings that for a brief moment come here to live these amazing lives, these gifts of learning that propel us to be the souls that we've dreamed of.

By improving who we are, we improve the lives of our loved ones.

EXPANSION OF THE MIND

How would you like to see yourself from a transformational point of view? Through the knowledge you've learned from these pages, you begin to see for yourself, that we are not alone in this game called life.

And if we call on our guides, our ancestors, we may see a progression in our lives, a new expansion in the way we think and see ourselves.

At the beginning of my transformation, I believe I was still in my primitive brain. I couldn't see the forest for the trees. I was the person stopping my expansion. I know that back then, I did not see myself as the evolved person I am. With William's love and guidance, I remembered who I was and this transformed me into the person I am today.

The knowledge of my past lives helped me. Catherine's quiet dignity, Lily's free-spirited thinking. They are a part of me. Both of them and many more lives taught me about myself. That's just it. We live these lives to learn about ourselves, and what we can discover about our soul in these journeys.

I couldn't be franker about what I'm going to say, in reconnection with who you truly are, you can see your own soul's progression, and it is eye-opening. Visiting the past can bring you into the present. It sounds simple, doesn't it? These guides, guides who truly see you for who you are can lead us to great places.

I would be remiss, if I didn't tell you what we need to do to progress our journey, to reconnect with who we really are. Close your eyes for a moment in a quiet place and accept the fact you are not alone.

Now ask this question, "Would someone like to speak to me?" You may get an answer, which pretty much sounds like your own thoughts. Take a closer look at that thought. We can train ourselves to learn to differentiate between our thoughts and theirs. I found this difficult at first and this is probably because I didn't trust what I was hearing. The more you practice, the better this will get, and eventually, you will be on your way to getting more messages.

Albert Einstein was a genius at this. He could quiet his mind enough that he began to pick up full conversations. He was better at it than most and called up a lot of information, information that helped him and a lot of others.

He accepted the idea of the theory of relativity as a gateway to transferred knowledge and almost unwittingly devised methods of transferring knowledge into logic. He could allay many transient numbers into basic numerical values, and in doing this it gave way to brilliant and not always-understood ideas.

Most saw it as bunk, as nonsense until the scientific world took notice and saw the genius this man had. He wouldn't have been able to produce such work without becoming a channel.

When push came to shove, Einstein was a remarkable intellect, however, the work he had done previous to his more famous work was dull in comparison. Most men do not have this ability to hear what is being said to them, because they are too in their heads to listen to these remarkable conversations of their ancestors.

In hearing this knowledge, he felt appreciative of what he was given, and even though it looked like he had this amazing brain, it was only because he had an open mind to what the universe could give in its secrets.

Wisdom does come from deep within. The wisest people have

devised ways to listen, listen to their hearts and minds. They trust what their gut is telling them.

I find when I'm annoyed with something, that I need to go to a quiet place and begin to examine what is the source of the irritation. Is it coming from me, or is it coming from another source? An empath can pick up on other people's feelings and emotions. I've devised ways to aid in this, through shielding meditations. My favorite, done in the yoga tree pose, is to draw positive energy from the earth, and then in my mind's eye, I begin to see this swirling energy rise up my body. I can see it become a cyclone of energy around me, a shield protecting me from outside energies, and as this swirling energy rises over my head, I send peace out into the universe.

This is a very powerful exercise I do daily.

Lining up my chakras is also something I do daily and this seems to help, although we have many chakras, doing a few will work wonders.

For people with mediumship abilities, it is important to keep up with your spiritual nature.

In collecting your daily thoughts, you should start the day balanced. I cannot say this enough, we as people who see farther than others can get stuck, if we don't pay attention to our spiritual health. Our light can steer those in the ghost world to us, and we can get drained of energy without knowing it. We are the master of our domain, and we cannot allow others with issues that have kept them from their true home to give us their dysfunction.

I make this clear when I deal with a lost soul.

We all want order in our lives and yet, I don't dismiss the pain of these wandering spirits.

I strongly believe I came into this life to be a soul rescuer. A psychologist to the world of the spirits who are not at rest. These spirits find themselves at odds with the life they lead and choose to stay behind for whatever reason. Maybe they were ripped from their life too soon, or possibly they do not know they are dead and can become trapped in a loop, a dimension lacking time and space.

A guide directed me to go to old Fort Sackville and to where a British General's ghost had been wandering the grounds since before the end of the Revolutionary War. Even though my spirit guide on this case was a general for the Americans during this time period, he felt this lost soul needed to come home.

That's just it, on the other side there is forgiveness, we are divine beings who are enlightened by the truth of who we are.

I said to this guide, "How is a British General going to respond to a woman from an advanced time, and how am I going to snap him out of this loop?"

The guide said this British officer had caused the deaths of many American troops, and still, I went. I shrugged my shoulders and got in my car and went to the George Roger's Clark Memorial. I walked up the path of the old French cemetery and asked if I could speak to a British Colonel. To my utter amazement, I immediately heard his English accent, and he believed me when I asked him if he remembered having dysentery, I then revealed he had passed away and had been walking the grounds for well over two hundred years. I asked him if it seemed like things were off and he agreed.

He was given the light and he went home.

Battlefields are some of my favorite places to go. The history is disturbing; however, the idea of releasing battle-worn troops gives me satisfaction, the satisfaction I have done my job.

Recently, I went with friends to a concert near Franklin Tennessee. The next day after the concert, we toured the old battlefield, where six thousand soldiers died during a five-hour siege.

I excused myself from my husband and friends and went to work.

I called them over and explained why I was there and asked if they were ready to go and most agreed. Thirty-five went over and six hung around, my spirit guide, William, revealed.

That evening, we went on a ghost walk and my friend and I caught some spirits on film, we later learned.

The last stop on the tour was an old house built before the Civil War had even come to Franklin. A beautiful, average size for its time, simplistic brick home with tall chimneys on either side. The tour guide told us the home was used for surgeries done to amputate limbs of wounded soldiers. Later, I viewed my friend's photo of me in the spot where the limbs would have been thrown out the window into a morbid pile. In the photo, everyone is clear except for me. To my surprise, I am enveloped in a hazy mist.

A little while later, I waited for my friends in front of a statue at the old town hall and asked if anyone else wanted to go home. William told me the six remaining soldiers had been following me and decided to take the same route their comrades had taken earlier in the day.

That old house stayed on my mind and before we left town the next morning, we returned. A story the guide told us the night before had me wondering if any other spirits were stuck.

The story happened before the war. A businessman built the two-bedroom home for his family and he spent more money on the grand house than he had. He devised a plan, a plan that would include his fifteen-year-old daughter. He found an older wealthy man for her to marry, way too old for her, a child. She did not want to marry this man and became so distraught the night before her wedding that she tied a bedsheet around the upstairs banister railing. Her parents heard the noise and came out of their room to a terrible sight, and to discover her body hanging from the two-story stairwell.

Some stories are forgotten to time, but this story resonated upstairs in the girl's bedroom.

In my mind's eye, I could see a young girl in a white gown with her knees pulled to her chest as she rocked herself to soothe her soon-to-be-come reality. I knew she had moved on to the other side long ago. I was transfixed in her room and didn't want to move. My friend, who also has abilities, and I went to the stairwell and again were moved back to the room.

The ghost was a man, her father, and in death had become stuck in his grief and guilt for causing his daughter so much pain. After her death, I could see him coming into her room and reliving that fateful night, and in death, he continued. That's why I felt so pulled into the room.

I began to communicate with the father on my journey around the house which is now a wonderful art gallery with the gallery owner and one of the artists working on site. They told us about the exhibits and being an art lover, I fell in love with this place.

In the exhibit room where the surgeries were done during the war, I began to get a headache anytime I was near the blood-stained floor and suddenly had a horrific residual vision of a young man on a table yelling that he didn't want to die.

As much as I didn't want to leave the gallery, with its beauty and tragic history, we had to be on the road toward Nashville for lunch with my cousin and her family.

We said our goodbyes to our friends, the gallery owner, and artist, and on the way out the door, I still tried to convince the father to move on. His daughter came to me and wanted him to go. In death, she'd forgiven him. I was getting in my car and told him it had to be now because I didn't want to be late for lunch with my cousin.

He and his daughter were reunited and my husband and I were late for lunch.

THE RESISTANT MIND

RESISTANCE IS THE HARDEST force.
If we find ourselves resistant to change, we can never discover who we truly are. Bending the mind just a little can be life-changing. Why do we adhere to such rigid structures of ourselves?

It's simply because the idea of change can be terrifying and in actuality, it can be life-changing. If we loosened the grip one iota, we can begin to see that it wasn't as hard as we thought. Now, I do know the pressures of life can keep us in its eternal grip, however, it is also that fear of the unknown that keeps us wrapped tightly in that snug blanket.

Sometimes I sound like I repeat myself, and this is only to bring direct knowledge to the surface. If we as an individual desire to behold the real vision of the truth, then we must seek others out in order to be the great teachers in life. To allow others in our lives is how we must find ourselves because if we remain static, we cannot learn.

I have met people in life who have become stagnant, who've become reclusive and I remember a time in my young life when I did not have the assurance that time has brought me. When I'm with others, I can see how I am represented. We all have moments of doubt in our lives and we need to take a look at these times and say to ourselves, if I were the only human on earth how could I learn, for without others, my life has little meaning.

When a young person finds themselves bullied, or possibly the object of scorn, it might make them fearful and this fear could hold them back from being who they truly are. They might be unsure of themselves, and not be comfortable with others, this will improve with age for most people go through this. It is just a foundation to get to adulthood, and sometimes it takes longer, however, if we allow these instances in our life to take control, we could become static and this would be a tragedy because we humans need other humans to feel complete, so for the introverted mind, we must say to ourself if for only a few minutes of the day, I get out of my comfort zone and then these small steps will eventually bring me greater joy. It's okay to be who we are, and whether we are extroverted or introverted, it is best to just be who you are and stop criticizing yourself.

We remain static, if you will, to such an idea that makes us tremble in fear, but what if the change we desire for our lives could lead us to something better? Perhaps more money, or a new self-image. Whatever it is you want, don't be afraid because the newfound luxury of getting out of our repetitive state can be life-altering.

Our ancestors knew about this, or we wouldn't be here. My own ancestors came over in a rickety boat called the Mayflower.

When I try to put myself in their shoes, I can't imagine giving up everything that was usually safe just because I wanted to pray the way I wanted. They defied death while many of their compadres did not, and this was probably desperation, and more than likely, ignorance. They faced mind-numbing cold living in the elements, expiring from disease, and becoming dependent on people who spoke not the same language, and definitely dressed in an entirely different fashion.

Would you face starvation to live the way you wanted? Genetically, we are designed to be like our ancestors. What has happened to that drive? We have become too comfortable in our lives to even begin to think of such a rash decision. There are many people still in this world who face starvation because of poverty, and wars, and to face it, just poor leadership.

Now I will get off my podium. I'm not even saying we need to cross an ocean to get to our hearts' desire. What I am saying is to get off that couch and do something. Contribute a little time to those less fortunate, and see what the universe gives in return.

I have afforded such luxuries in my life to ascertain that my own life had become static, so I decided to follow the path of least resistance. Someone said many years ago, and I would be remiss if I didn't say, we get what we give in this life.

If we can envision a life without trials and tribulations, then we can envision a life that has been put on hold. We can develop a new way of thinking, merely by taking a step toward the creation of our own desire. We can look in the mirror and say to ourselves, I am not here to remain static, I am here for something bigger than myself.

Contributing is the only way to get out of one's head. Contribute to a charity cause for a couple of days a week. Walk dogs for an animal shelter, or help dish out mashed potatoes at a soup kitchen, whatever you do, try and get a little out of your comfort zone.

I resign myself to say, that giving a little in my life won't hurt me, however, it could help someone else.

If we can look at the big picture of why we are here, then we can eliminate those obstacles holding us back. A good general picture of why we are here is because we desire to get out of the comfort of our true home to come to a place that can be rife with trials, and learning experiences.

Thirty-some years ago, one of my favorite television shows was called Quantum Leap. A brilliant scientist, Sam Beckett, leaps into the lives of all sorts of people and is aided by the hologram of his friend, Al. They try to make history better for individuals from different time periods. A few days ago, I rediscovered reruns of this old show, and it made me think, isn't this sort of want we are doing here, jumping through the lives of different characters? Why not play these parts well? If we are going to make this quantum jump through a wormhole, then why not make it your best?

They aren't too far off on the quantum leap theory. We are in essence jumping through lives in an incredible amount of quantum energy. This field of massive amounts of energy that propels our souls through space and time to live a life intended for good, and for learning.

Isn't it intriguing the fact we are here, to begin with, and if we can learn how and why, it paints an entirely different view of own existence.

Quantum physics can explain how we got here with a little stretching of the mind, and lessons in science; however, why are we here? This question eludes most of us.

We have probably wondered why would we put ourselves through such rigorous lives filled with danger and hard work, and I can answer that question. You have leaped into the life you are living now because these lives fascinate us. The lives of our ancestors are incredible stories, some we know, and some we don't. It's just we experience the lives of our ancestors through their eyes, a telling of what got us here in the first place. They can tell so much if we just listen.

I found myself studying the history of my family and thought to myself, they had such cleverness, such forethought. I am here because of them, and what they went through.

My own grandfather was a mechanic, not a high-powered person, but one with ingenuity. I understood from his brother-in-law, that he designed an engine that someone else got credit for. Well, we all have lives where others get credit for what we do. It's not the end of the world by any means, however, he knew what he did, and in the end that's all that truly matters.

Wisdom does come from within, and I would be remiss if I did not share this with you.

Kristianne Ferrier

On speaking of successes, I did find other inventive ancestors. My great-grandfather, Charles Ferrier for instance, created these beautiful large late-century church doors. He sold produce from a wagon he designed with removable side panels to reveal benches of wonderful vegetables grown from his large acreage of land. His ingenuity was noticed by Henry Ford and he was hired as one of Ford's main carpenters. His work can be viewed at the Henry Ford Museum in Detroit which he helped build.

My grandmothers were extremely good cooks and fabulous seamstresses. I've still got some of their crocheted tablecloths.

Our ancestors leave a legacy given to us. We can move forward in our lives in order to leave the next generations with remarkable stories, no matter how simple, or how profound.

THE WARRIOR MIND

THE WARRIOR MIND FEELS invincible. It's the part of us that says we can conquer the world. It represents that part of us that contains some of the DNA from our ancestors. It says I am a central part of my being that will not take any guff from anyone.

If you value yourself as a warrior-minded person, you might see far deeper than most. It's only when you find yourself in crisis that fight comes to life. The warrior mind compliments the lymphatic system.

In the logical-minded individual, they will have that fight or flight emotion, however, in the warrior-minded person they will be ready for a fight. In a person who is not as evolved as some, this can lead to a problematic situation when they are mentally ready for a fight.

Not all warrior-minded people lose their cool, for the balanced individual, there is common sense. They use their judgment in these intense situations.

When speaking of the ancestors, they probably had more of these situations occur in their lives. Were they trained more to prepare for these disasters? I think not, although many of them conquered fear and kept a cool head about them, especially going into battle.

Some of mine were warriors. They were soldiers, some were generals, and some were Native American warriors. Whatever they were, they wore their pride high. They saw themselves as something bigger, as part of a whole, whether they lost their lives, like my 10th great-grandfather, Dr. Rowland, who lost his battle by speaking against the Catholic Church. He was given an education by King Henry the 7th and burned at the stake by orders from Henry's granddaughter, Bloody Queen Mary, during the time of the English Reformation.

He had a warrior mind because he refused to take his ideals back. He stood for a cause and died for it, and this mindset was genetic because many of his ancestors took the same road.

They stood for the fight of a new nation, they fought for the enslavement of a people, and they didn't back down.

I have often felt the inborn instinct from them. That fight. Some of this comes from them, and some of it comes from my incarnations, for one time, I was up in the middle of the night and heard my grandmother's voice say, "You were once a Carthaginian General." My head began to spin, a what or who, I thought. I'd heard about the Carthaginians in history but knew nothing about them. So, I thought, I lived a male life. Not surprisingly, I understood many of us lived the lives of the opposite sex. I wanted to know more about this fellow and began to do research.

Several names popped up on my computer, and one seemed more noticeable than the others, and my guides said yes. This man had been crushed by the loss of his army and went into seclusion and died of starvation. The warrior mind can be great, but it can also be fallible.

For years I said, I was born with a sword in my hand. Well, apparently so.

THE UNPROVOKED MINDSET

I F WE HAVE DECIDED that the unseen world minds its own business, then I hate to say you are sorely mistaken, how about I say, let's take a look at facts.

This is about the brilliant scientists, artists, and writers who came before us. These men and women who produced such amazing knowledge for the world, could it be it came from another source? I've already mentioned Einstein, and Tesla, of course, their contributions have been unlimited.

Let's take a look at another. How about Edgar Cayce? His influence came from a source we do not recognize. Called the Sleeping Prophet, he would go into a trance-like state, and give his patients the medical knowledge he received from somewhere. Could he have been a secret genius without formal education? I think not. He did cure many a patient and became a phenom the world hasn't seen since. People believe these messages he received came from our true home, heaven. And if you find this hard to believe, I understand. Science has yet to give credence to this type of thing. We simply nod our heads in confusion and move on to the next.

If we did take more notice of these men who received transferred knowledge, could we not say to ourselves, well just maybe, we could do it. What if you decided you wanted to channel one of the great minds from the evolution of time? Could we not do it?

Like Edgar Cayce, is it possible to put ourselves into a meditative state of mind and give others the transferred information that could help us?

Well, I cannot give you a dignified answer to that, so I will say, why not?

We remember ourselves as young once, and we represent that moment in time when all was new, and all seemed possible. This was usually not a time of great strife, however, a moment of prolonged events that transformed our lives into who we are today. Not just an unfamiliarized person, but one of great courage, and beneficial to the human race, the human genome.

I encourage the reader to remember a time, a time in which you were given life lessons you needed to move forward. An example for others, so to speak, an example of what others deemed you to be.

I also encourage you to allow your mind to take yourself to task, and create a vision of the remarkable moments of your early life. A life purpose that you chose to be part of.

An event in your early life could have easily set you off track to the trajectory of your aim. Why did this event shape you? Did it encourage you, or did it divide you into someone you did not intend to be? I can suffer the consequences of such events to the preliminary results it should have had in my young life. I commend you if you were able to pull yourself up by the bootstraps to such life-changing events.

Now, why do some suffer from early happenings? Why do they become defeated and allow themselves to take on issues that are beyond their control? I will tell you this, if you are left to take on the tragedies of this world, then you will become sad and complex to the point of no return. Now it might sound like I repeat myself. I in no way wish individuals to take on the weight of the world. Those who do will defeat themselves.

Let us look back on this child of God we were, and see ourselves in an event that could be holding us back. Now, put yourself in the mindset of going back to that moment, and then back to the present. Do you see how this event shaped you? Would you want that child to take on the weight of something beyond their control? In the present, what do you see? You are an adult with choices, and you can take that child's hand and give them comfort, the comfort maybe they did not receive. Lift yourself up. You are in control now, and you sympathize with your younger self and can lead them in a new way, a way that is not self-defeating. You are your own future, a future that can be rife with difficulties, but a future that can have great promise.

THE EXPERIMENTAL MIND

T HIS PERSON FINDS THEMSELVES looking at everything under a microscope. They systematically evaluate everything in their path. An undervalued experimental-minded person could find they are at odds with themselves.

What makes a person so inclined to debunk everything? I will tell you this, they are intrinsically of the mindset they want to solve the world's problems, and in doing this, they can find their way. This person is the opposite of the trivial-minded person. They will objectify all in their path.

If you find yourself in the realm of one of these fine people, they will solve anything you need solved, for they are so adept at coming to conclusions, that they are typically rated as a genius.

If they become limited in their workspace, they will invariably find another place to do their studies. With the human genome, these individuals will categorize themselves as a first-rate mastermind. I have rarely met this personality type, but would find myself in good company.

My spirit guide, and 4th Great-Grandfather, William, who I've mentioned before, was of the experimental mind. He liked to have his head in a book and received the rank of Surgeon General during the War of 1812. A psychic friend saw him teaching surgery on a riverboat.

If we can say, we are a person who desires to study and

figure things out, then there is a good chance you are this gifted personality type.

In categorizing our personality then maybe we'll see an ancestor who was like us. Are you a gifted musician? If we look far enough back, like my musician son, we will probably find an ancestor with our same talent.

As I said earlier, I am a medium, and I am definitely not the first in my family, nor will I be the last. We have a long genetic strand if we take a look at it. Could it go back to the time of Adam and Eve? Well maybe, if they truly existed, then we all would.

Take a look at the human race. We are all intertwined in one way or another. If we understood the concept of how we are more alike than different, we would begin to see we have more similarities than not. We focus too much on skin color, religion, and other things that set us farther away from our fellow compatriots. Our human desire to judge can be our downfall. Has there ever been a time in history when we all just got along? Maybe, if we could see back before written history.

Back to the experimental mind.

You are an individual with the capacity to bring hope into the world. If you are a scientist, could you bring hope to the millions and create a cure for a life-ending disease?

Take cancer for instance. Haven't great minds already devised methods to cure this devastating disease? If we only knew. They have. They have found the reason why some people get this many times incurable disease. If the person with cancer doesn't treat the maladies from their diet and exercise, they cannot and will not get rid of this dreaded illness. Some individuals have the genetic genome for cancer, and beating it has everything to do with lifestyle, diet, and exercise. The disease can be treated with diet, and what you put in your mouth.

We will find, that in treating cancer, we can change the process of the mutation of cells. It isn't so ingenious to figure this out. They've known for some time and didn't let it out to the mainstream population for fear of losing funding for drugs. The reason cancer still kills is because of bureaucracy. The people in charge are so focused on money, they've forgotten they have the answers. Isn't this the issue with many things in life? That we know the answers. It is only because of the money trail that we still contend with life-altering problems.

Take hunger, for example. There is enough food in this world. We just don't have enough people to take it to task. The leaders in this world are so engrossed in fighting and being right, that they forget about the multitudes of people who got them in office.

Leaders need to live by this motto.

I am an example to the people I lead. If I cannot represent them in a way that is nurturing, then I have forgotten why I decided to lead in the first place.

IN THE MIND OF DIVINE INTERVENTION

I F WE COULD TAKE a look at divine intervention for a moment. We could see the complexities in the very idea. When we think of the word, it takes us back to religion, and the idea of miracles that can come from God, Mother Mary, or any other fabulous deities that are out there. I have long transformed the idea of a true miracle to other higher souls. Could it be that our ancestors can make things happen for their loved ones on earth?

If I could prescribe to you a thought, a thought that is intricate to the very idea of a genuine miracle. Take a look at your own life. Do you have any memories of something that has happened to you that was too good to be true? This incident does not have to be earth-shattering and make you raise your arms to the sky in delight. It can be simple. It can be something as simple as being in the right place at the right time.

We may shrug off the idea that this is some lucky incident that left us a little richer inside, or possibly money-wise. Could it be possible that Uncle Joe looked down from his heavenly home and deemed it upon himself to do a little and help aid his family below?

We may never know, but the idea can be a little nice that they still think about us in our earthly existence.

Again, I go back to the theory of relativity for an example only

121

because it explains so much. Our divine principles and organized theories go hand in hand. We achieve the greatest by becoming the very people we dreamed up once upon a time. Now I'll clue you in. The idea of miracles can cause you to think, did I help someone else in need, in other words by doing a good deed, could I have gotten some help from the other side? I imagine we have thought about this from time to time. And I will tell you, yes, we do get divine help from giving selflessly.

It may be something small as giving a few dollars to someone standing on a street corner, or to helping an elderly person cross the street. The meaning of this is simple, we are not here for ourselves. We are here to set an example for others. The true meaning of life is to show kindness to one another.

In this time and place in history, I don't see a lot of that going on. People are very into their tight-woven lives to even smile and say hello. As an example, a few days ago my husband and I were walking on a narrow path and moved to give another couple the right of way. Not because niceness is a weakness, but it's a kindness to give a little courtesy. Although we said hello, the lack of smiles and acknowledgment made me think, have we become so uncomfortable with others, we find ourselves too subdued to even crack a smile? Have we become too complacent with our fellow man?

Maybe though, they argued and were too angry to even nod. I have to laugh, I analyze everything.

People shop at their least favorite shopping chain. I won't give out its name, some refer to it as Wally World. It's so convenient because they have everything. Being an empath, I try to avoid shopping there. The energy is terrible only because others feel that same way. People glare at you if you're in their path, and I suspect some customers would run you over with their cart if they could without going to jail.

People have become so put off by others that they have

become this race of lackluster individuals. Mind you, there are a few angels out there.

If we could take the time to see what we put out into the universe, maybe, just maybe the universe would give back.

I rest my case.

THE CURIOUS MIND
OF THE THEORY
OF RELATIVITY

I HAVE LONG THEORIZED THIS idea, the idea of the theory of relativity as you can see in my previous chapters because it is so versatile. If we continue to use this as an example, we will see that all is not what it seems in our ability to do what is needed, and we will see the scope of time.

As I read this back to myself, I realized this may not resonate with others, however, in the long run, this paragraph is far more reaching than we know and not filler that is intended to get to my quota of words.

As humans, we tend to evaluate everything in our path, some more than others. A complete sentence would look like this. If I trade my way of thinking for a moment, I will see my judgment is one of a critical eye, and if I truly value myself as a human, and how I perceive others, then I will begin to see how others might judge me. Who deemed us to be the critic, the critical eye that sees the flaws in others? Did they deserve that judgment? I think not, for the perceiving eye is not seeing the full picture.

Critical theory is one of the most profound ways of giving a name to things, things that are not within reach of our understanding. I liken this to a tree. A tree is not only alive, but it is also very unique. Its branches twist and turn like no other tree, for isn't this the way of a human?

Even identical twins have their own uniqueness about them for the sharpest eye to see, for each individual on the planet is unique in their own way, and once we begin to see this, we see that our judgment is not needed.

Recently, I joined my dad for lunch at his assisted living care facility, when a woman, younger than the people who live there, sat down with us. Debra clearly had a disability. Now the men at the table wouldn't look at her and snickered as she repeated herself pretty consistently, kind of reminded me of a parrot, not that this is a judgment about her. I found her to have a positive attitude in her constant statements. She found her food very good, and initially when I introduced myself and later said goodbye, her response was genuine. I have rarely felt that when someone said it was nice to meet you, there was such genuine, heartfelt sincerity behind it.

After I left the building, I felt like I had met a beautiful person, this person, who others categorized as simple, was far more than could meet the eye. If a decerning eye could see deeper, then they would understand, she was much more than her disability.

I have learned in my nearly sixty years of existence to look at people the way I would like them to see me, as a flawed human, however, as a person who is valuable.

Some of the chain of events in my life have not always been easy, but I've tried to look at life in a positive way, a creative way. Life was not meant to be easy, it is meant to be lessons, lessons that may not be easy, however, they will teach us if we are lucky, to be the best person we can be. And if that is not thought-provoking, then I don't know what is.

In evaluating others, we can understand each person has something to give, even the common criminal has value. If we look at that person who has chosen an illicit life, we can pretty much look at the individual who was not valued as a child, and probably, if we could see their early life, we would cringe.

Our culture has deemed the criminal population as not deserving, not deserving of a better life. Is it too late to show these people compassion, the compassion they didn't receive in their formative years?

There are some people from not-so-good neighborhoods, neighborhoods others try to avoid, where they are taught at a young age to steal everything that is not tied down. Now others find this reprehensible that people will steal from them, and they will see it as an offense that someone has the gall to take what you have worked so hard for.

Now, the criminal mind undervalues itself so much that they feel work is a bad word. Why work when you can just take? If this is alright, alright in your culture, then this individual will say to himself, why not do what you see?

The criminal mind is made, it is not drawn out of a hat.

Back to the ancestors, they worked hard, most came into the country legally and made their way, sometimes to riches and sometimes to poverty, and whichever your family did, probably made you who you are today.

Now back to the individual person, the unique individual who is made up of cells, neurons, and molecules, aren't we all made the same? We come born into this world a living breathing whole human being who has the making of a person who can do anything, anything they desire, but that road can instantly turn if we are born to people, people who have not made the most out of their life, people who have been conditioned from the start to not be able to come out of poverty, poverty of the mind.

THE METAPHYSICAL MIND

W HEN WE SPEAK OF the metaphysical mind, we might refer
to the writings of James Frederick Ferrier, who I'm told is
a distant cousin of mine. This Scottish-born genius was born to
be brilliant. He deciphered more than one equation of the mind.
I cannot say enough about the contributions this man-made, for
surely, he was ahead of his time.

This man coined the idea of the metaphysical, and if you
look at his writings, which are taught today at some mainstream
universities, you will see he was no trivial man. My eyes crossed
trying to decipher his meanings.

Now if we look into what his deep understandings meant, we
can see he could go farther than the typical man's mind can go.
Could it be he also channeled from the great minds of where we
come from?

I can give you the gist of what he was saying. He was taking
the parts of the human mind and giving them a name. He simply
wanted to understand the reasons why we thought the way we
do. A deep thinker often takes a look at the intricate processes
of the congruousness mind. If you value yourself as one of these
thinkers, you will say to yourself, why do I think this way, why
do I gravitate to things others do not?

This is important because it teaches us our values. Our value
systems give way to modern thinking. Not just the getting-by

mindset that many of our ancestors had, however, we are a product of our imagination.

In mainstream science, we categorize things, we give them a name, and this name is what gives us equations, and these equations are what give us our finished product. So, if we scientifically look at the mind, we will begin to see our function, our function that makes us human. We can become a statistic, a product of who we are.

James Ferrier categorized the individual areas of the brain, these parts that give us function. If we are of two minds, then we function as a whole. We are more than our brain power, we come from some higher form of purpose, an evolved unlimited people with a human brain that can take us farther than we can process. This is good. It shows us we are more than the undervalued species we have sometimes limited ourselves to be. We are more than the wars and things we have done to each other on a destructive path through world history.

If we limit ourselves to be this race of hostile individuals, we will eventually destroy our chances of taking our civilization to an extreme understanding, and to a society of great learning potential. In learning we are more; we can see for ourselves as having been limited to the status of the unevolved human.

By connecting with our ancestors, they can remind us of who we are, not of who we've become because, in the long run, we are so much more.

Divide and conquer.

Could this be the answer? Not divide and conquer our enemies, however, to separate our ways of thinking, to become a part of evolved thinkers. These men and women who do not allow mainstream society to tell them who to be. They decide, they decide to be great instead of allowing others to dictate who they should be.

I want to go back to the undervalued. These people in society who have limited themselves, frankly, I no longer see myself as one of them. When I began to see farther than I used to, and it became apparent, I had been raised to be this way. My parents, who were not always great parental guides, and had children because that's what you did back then, taught us to be open-minded thinkers, whether they knew it or not.

Even though I did not have the best education living in a rural area, we still had a library in our home, a library of the classics, of science, and books that made you think. I remember at a young age my mother taking us by the hand to the local library. I grew up loving to read.

I began to understand what you read and put into your mind is how you see life. If we read the books that make us think, then we will become individuals who have potential, potential to create greatness, like in the works of James Frederick Ferrier, who also wanted to be a keynote speaker in this book.

He said to me, "I can attest to you that I am no figment of your imagination. I am the real deal, and yes, we are distant cousins on your dad's father's side."

In speaking about the metaphysical, I can correctly say, that it has changed its value from what I was originally teaching, which was the correlation between logic and reason.

If we have logic and reason on our side, then we can produce a genius mind for when we have these objective parts of us, then we can truly become the actor we proclaim to be in our life.

If you ascribe yourself to be reasonable and capable, then these two parts of your mind can be in harmony, and you will be able to contain a molecular structure of autonomy in your daily grind. If this seems above your head, then I will make it easier to understand by saying, consciously aware of these two components, can take the primitive brain to task.

If you deliver your way of thinking into words that eliminate any divisive way of contributing to the productive realm of existing in a world that is so far-flung, we forget to stay on course. In eliminating any doubts about your existence, you can see we all have an exterior that is far superior to any known species on Earth.

When we understand the miracle of the brain and its purpose, then we can know what we are capable of, and not just some inferior species that inhabit the earth. We have the capacity to learn, instinct, and drive, which increases our chance for success on the Earth plane. We conceive that for a species of relatively unknown origins, we either come from ape to man, or from some other unknown but existing worlds.

I find that humans have intellectually dumbed themselves down for the purpose of fitting in, which by my theory, is a cop-out.

There once was a time when man thought nothing of using the English language for how it was designed to be used, and not in slang, or some inferior way of communicating. We had knowledge of intellect, books written by the greats of their time, to the inferior reproduction of these books used for smut. I wouldn't advise reading one. Look for the classics, look for the books that have meaning, and a storyline that can speak volumes through the ages.

THE GELATINOUS
MOLD OF THE MIND

I HAVE LONG PROGRAMMED MYSELF to speak the truth and this has given me a chance to see things for how they really are. If we incorporate justice in our lives, we receive back, what we give. Give and take, so to speak.

I wondered about a person's life span and the incredible amount of time we incorporate into our daily functions. In regards to this, I have held myself to higher standards in some ways, and let the important things flounder. It's easy to do. We're all guilty of it, and that's why we leave this plane never accomplishing the things we intended to do.

If we don't allow time for the things we love doing, then we are just going through the motions, and how sad is this? Even if it's buying a motorcycle and traveling the open roads, then take time to do this. Traveling and seeing other things is wonderful, it takes the mind to new heights. I've met people who are afraid of traveling, of getting out and seeing the world, and mind you, the world is a dangerous place, however, for the most part, it is safe, and very few people meet their deaths by the hands of someone not stable.

Now back to the part about my abilities, and to diseased thought processes.

When we review our lives, we become aware of things we did to ourselves, and others that were not exactly refined. So, in reviewing these things it does help us grow, however, if we sinned against mankind, we may find ourselves in hot water. Say you murdered someone, maybe you murdered more than one person, then you may ask, what happens to a soul who murdered someone in cold blood?

Well, I can tell you this, chances are this soul will remain as an earthbound spirit.

I wouldn't give anyone the benefit of the doubt here, but your existence on the Earth plane is for learning and not taking advantage of others. If we are of the mindset to take, chances are you could become earthbound.

I gave this chapter the name gelatinous mold of the mind because I dealt with such a thing. Now our minds might go to an old movie called The Blob, simply because that's what it was, a blob that would go around devouring people. Well, now this sounds like nonsense, however, as fantastic as this sounds, one of these things came into my house.

My son, also a medium, became a target of a highly negative entity one evening. I asked St. Michael to escort away this malevolent ghost, and later, I heard my guide, William, say to me, "You have a gelatinous mold in your living room."

"A what," I exclaimed. "That sounds disgusting, and why would this thing be moldering in my living room."

William was concerned because this thing was the remains of this ghost, and this blob could thoroughly put a household into bedlam. In St. Michael's haste to remove this ghost, it had left that hideous part of itself behind, while I understand from my guides this is rare, this ghost had been a murderer in life, who had gotten away with slaying three people in our area.

I was reminded of a murder-suicide back in the late seventies that I had completely forgotten about and told this act was done by this man who was this bad spirit, and not the husband, as everyone thought. This unfortunate couple's daughter had been in my sister's class in school. Another one of this man's victims had been a young girl in another county, which resulted in an innocent person being incarcerated.

I was not given the name of this murderer, and since it's been so long ago, my only concern was to remove this blob. With the help of St. Michael and my son's angel, Edward, the energy was destroyed.

This sick individual had killed three people in life, and his ghost was still destructive. This type of spirit can cause people with medium tendencies, especially the young, to become depressed, suicidal, or worse. I liken these cold-blooded killers to evolved evil energy that can continue on the path to the destruction of humans.

So, you ask, why is this important to know, and I will tell you that if you suddenly become depressed and feel like you are hearing voices in your head, you may not be delusional, it could be you have unknown abilities, and an evil ghost has attached itself to you. Of course, this knowledge is out there, but it does make you wonder how many people have been deemed mentally ill, or possibly schizophrenic when in all actuality they had been possessed.

From time to time, as I said before, occasionally, I will deal with one of these spirits who lived a depraved life, and who I am not afraid of, maybe they should be afraid of me.

Now, the other kind, the kind that has not lived a human life. These can be a little trickier to get rid of, however, they can also be dispelled which sometimes takes great effort. I warrant you, that a person not skilled in this should probably call in someone who has dealt with them, a priest, or a demonologist. Few people have actually gone to battle with the devil, so to speak, and won. I find the challenges to be exhilarating, maybe I have a little of the daredevil in me after all, although I do have to laugh because I scream for my husband if I see a spider.

Now on to happier things. I find life interesting, maybe more so in this life because I know this is my last life in the earth school.

In the event of my passing someday, I hope that I have helped alleviate the concerns others have in their lives, being this is a big reason for this book. We are transformed by knowledge, knowledge that those of our future generations, could have access to the truth.

I would not say, I am the premier educator who knows the truth. However, I have consulted, I have studied and channeled those who have given me the knowledge of the ages. For in the ages of man, we will find ourselves, and not just the memories of those who come before us, but from the ashes of time, for written in these ashes are the divine knowledge of the human race.

PROLOGUE

The Search for William

You might have heard me mention my guide, William, in my book. I wanted to give him credit because, without William, there would be no book.

In my search through historical records, I found him, and in him, I found myself. A love story that has tested time. I have always heard of soul mates, but never thought too much about it.

When I remembered who he was, and remembered our life together as my 4th great-grandparents over two hundred years ago, it brought such a profound change in me and reminded me of new old knowledge that says our lives are not static.

I had dreams, dreams of a handsome man stalking me, and of that same man helping me up on a small brown horse. We were everything to each other.

I've written romance novels, and none could touch the love of Will and Cathy. Will's mother, Grandma Sarah, said the two of them took your breath away, so even though we are physically away from each other, our minds are still in sync. He has not left my side since he left his last life as an engineer named, Mark, twenty-years ago. I understood those years ago, I gained a male guide, it just took me years to figure it out, and he reminds me every day that we are of one mind, not a single soul is more in tune than us.

I call him by the name I called him in our earth life together. He has told me what his fifth-dimensional name is. He is Erad, pronounced Airad. I am Evalane.

So, I wanted to leave you with the profound knowledge if you are not with your soul mate at this moment, in the blink of an eye, and in the scope of time, you will be together, again.

In all our incarnates, we can develop ourselves enough that we can say, I don't need any further earth school lessons. For those who desire to continue, will surely give it another try.

Many of the recent incarnates have decided on their last time on earth. They represent a large amount of the individuals who have completed what they intended to learn or have been so turned off by the earth school, they have decided they've had enough.

I don't see my lives as a waste of time, I see them as a contribution to the scope of time.

Sadly, as this book was coming to completion, my father passed and went to our heavenly home. Although a solemn moment, my view on death saw this as a happy time.

His words to me were to be sure to take care of these fractures before you come home. He also went on to tell me what heaven is like.

This place draws you into a new path that leaves you in dismay. I cannot even describe it. It is a whole lot of souls and we all work together, and some are more passionate about certain things. The libraries are filled with so much information, you cannot even imagine. There is no discord here. We try to work things out and are logical about it. This place called heaven is immense. When we die, we truly go home. It's incredible here. We don't thirst, we don't need food to sustain us, just tons of knowledge about the universe and everything that has ever been.

We all take pieces of our lives here; however, we don't necessarily keep them unless we leave a portion of ourselves on Earth. Another thing is we produce art and literature to be given to those on earth who can channel.

There are more important things you should know. This is a time for deep reflection on my life, and I am given time to do this. It isn't always easy, and I know I didn't always do the right thing. I just wish I'd known more. We don't go through life without bumps and bruises. We cherish the ones who we leave behind, and once we get home, we stay close to the ones we've gone through lives with before.

If I had this knowledge, my life would have been a lot different.

We work at going through our life trauma. We can be traumatized by things we didn't even realize. Things that may seem small, aren't really. There are groups of people that meet together to discuss their traumas. Kind of like AA. We don't trivialize the damage these lives can do to us. They can victimize us to the point, we need a type of therapy. If I were all of you, I would deal with those things as soon as possible because the longer it goes on, the more difficult. We do work with those who were part of that earthly trauma. It can be very healing. We all work for the good of others. It's not just about ourselves here. If you keep your traumas in, they can become almost stagnant.

Many veterans of war have to go through a type of therapy. We get past these lives, then we can move on, and continue the work we do.

Dad shared with me the book, Chariots of the Gods, back in the 70's, and even though I was young, I began to share his interest.

The pyramids were originally built as grids to produce energy. Some weren't built for this; however, most were built universally for spaceship landing pads. They would recharge and take off. They needed a place to fuel, and that is why there are so many similar structures. They reproduced them all over the world. Many of the early dynasties were aware of other worlds and really didn't view them the way modern man does. It was just part of the world order of things. Different species interacted with other species. Some pyramids were built by humans, and some weren't.

Those who viewed these otherworldly beings as Gods, built them in reverence. They did not realize the Gods were actually aliens from other worlds.

We are divine beings. None of us are trivial. We're all divine. Travel well, Dad, for you are now with the ancestors.

William

Printed in the United States
by Baker & Taylor Publisher Services